Reading, Writing, *and* Queer Survival

Reading, Writing, *and* Queer Survival

AFFECTS, MATTERINGS, AND
LITERACIES ACROSS APPALACHIA

CALEB PENDYGRAFT

A note to the reader: This volume contains discussions of sensitive topics, including sexual assault and substance-use disorder, as well as quotations containing anti-LGBTQ+ language. Discretion is advised.

Copyright © 2025 by The University Press of Kentucky

Scholarly publisher for the Commonwealth, serving Bellarmine University, Berea College, Centre College of Kentucky, Eastern Kentucky University, The Filson Historical Society, Georgetown College, Kentucky Historical Society, Kentucky State University, Morehead State University, Murray State University, Northern Kentucky University, Spalding University, Transylvania University, University of Kentucky, University of Louisville, University of Pikeville, and Western Kentucky University.
All rights reserved.

Editorial and Sales Offices: The University Press of Kentucky
663 South Limestone Street, Lexington, Kentucky 40508-4008
www.kentuckypress.com

Library of Congress Cataloging-in-Publication Data

Names: Pendygraft, Caleb, author.
Title: Reading, writing, and queer survival : affects, matterings, and
   literacies across Appalachia / Caleb Pendygraft.
Description: Lexington, Kentucky : The University Press of Kentucky,
   [2025] | Series: Appalachian futures: Black, native, and queer voices |
   Includes bibliographical references.
Identifiers: LCCN 2024056938 | ISBN 9781985902411 (hardcover ; alk.
   paper) | ISBN 9781985902428 (paperback ; alk. paper) | ISBN
   9781985902435 (pdf) | ISBN 9781985902442 (epub)
Subjects: LCSH: Queer theory—Appalachian Region. | Literacy—
   Appalachian Region—Philosophy.
Classification: LCC HQ76.25 .P448 2025 | DDC
   304.2/808660974—dc23/eng/20250131
LC record available at https://lccn.loc.gov/2024056938

*For all the queer kinships that persist in the world,
including the nonhumans who can teach
us to live kinder lives*

Contents

Prologue: When Mountains Get Up and Leave   ix
 1. Animacy, Literacy, and Queer Agency   *1*
 2. Queer Appalachia and Queer Stories   *23*
 3. Matters of the Closet   *49*
 4. Queer Affinities   *73*
 5. Carrying Mountains to the Sea   *109*

Acknowledgments   *133*
Appendix: Interview Questions and Consent Form   *139*
Notes   *147*
About the Author   *161*

Prologue
When Mountains Get Up and Leave

From his oversized recliner, post morning-insulin shot, my papaw asked me, "Kay-lup"—he didn't have his dentures in—"do you really believe if you prayed hard enough and had faith the grain of a mustard seed, you could move that mountain out there?" He, of course, was talking about the hill and lake outside. The one he made after carving out Appalachian humus and earth, leveling the side of the Kentucky knob enough to build my grandparents' house. Granny was in front of her well-seasoned cast-iron skillets, frying bacon and eggs, whisking gravy with a fork. The smell of biscuits rose from the stove through her muumuu and met me sitting on the floor in front of my dad's dad. I knew Papaw was asking about Matthew 17:20.

"Yeah, Papaw. I believe. Jesus said we can do it."

"Then I want you to pray and see if you can move that one." He pointed outside.

At the time, I did pray. And each time I came to visit, I'd look at the oversized wooden steps that led up to the lake my dad and my papaw shaped with machine and sweat, and I'd pray again. I believed as much as my ten-year-old body would allow.

I prayed for another year, give or take a season, till I'd look at the hillside and my papaw for the last time. I quit praying. I quit visiting. I quit being straight. I quit allowing myself to be beat by my father. It wasn't till eight years later, when I was plagued by a series of night sweats and horrific dreams, that I'd return. Every time I'd fall asleep, I was back in my papaw and granny's house, but the house wasn't the same. There wasn't a floor, and a deep abyss was circling outside. Granny would acknowledge I was with her in this dreamscape, but Papaw was missing. All I wanted was to get to my granddad. The nightmares continued in various reels of sleep. In my waking life, I hadn't spoken to that side of the family in years, but I was determined to travel, see Papaw, and kill the dreams. I drove through a massive flood in the spring of 2008; a trailer floated alongside the road at some point as I made my way through the Kentucky knobs. When I arrived at my grandparents' home, Granny was sweeping the debris from the storm off the patio.

"Hey, Granny!"

Her eyes winced, trying to make out the strange visitor on her land. "Caleb?" I want to say I remember her covering her mouth in shock. "Oh my!"

We wept together, and within minutes, I told her I came to see Papaw.

"You didn't hear?" she asked. "We buried him yesterday."

Later I'd tell her about how I'd came out and I couldn't come around them anymore because they didn't agree with that lifestyle. I looked around and noticed that the lake and hill were excavated. The mountain got up and left for some reason I still don't know. Later, the dreams stopped.

A literacy scholar may read my narrative above and claim my grandparents were literacy sponsors for me. *Literacy sponsor* is a common phrase in literacy studies, credited to Deborah Brandt's definition as "any agents, local or distant, concrete or abstract, who enable, support, teach, and model, as well as recruit, regulate, suppress, or withhold, literacy—and gain advantage by it in some way."[1] My papaw in particular fits well into this definition. He acted then as an agent in my immediate world who supported my reading of the Bible. When he questions my faith, he alludes to a deeper connection he and I had as being part of the same religious context—and while he perhaps wouldn't agree, he did gain advantage by spreading his faith to his grandson, as did the religion. Outside of my story, I can tell you that he regulated what I could watch and see on TV and cautioned against reading *Harry Potter*. He even "read" my hair and clothes as inappropriate on church Sundays. In short, he was indeed a literacy sponsor. No question.

Nevertheless, I find that conventional notions of literacy sponsorship fail to account for all the complexities of meaning-making and power relations in queer lives. And while literacy sponsorship isn't the only apparatus used to measure and ascertain an individual's literacy, it does reveal that it's oft the case that literacy scholarship tends to emphasize humancentric approaches to literacy. It's for this reason this project works to expand the scope of literacy, to further efforts to include nonhuman actors in our understanding of literacy and pay attention to affects produced from literacy practices. Animacy can be described as "a quality of agency, awareness, mobility, and liveness," and I suggest there are nonhuman, underexplored elements of literacy and literacy sponsors that animate us.[2] By *us*, I'm not simply speaking of individuals and the literacy they possess. To invoke the argument that "human beings are with and of the earth, and the biotic and abiotic powers of this earth are the main story," literacy involves an amalgam of the human and nonhuman, organic and inorganic, stretching across a spectrum from concrete materiality to the abstraction of belief.[3] What would happen if we were to reconsider literacy as acting outside the human-to-human interactions? What if affects, beliefs, and the inanimate actually do animate our literacy practices? *Reading, Writing, and Queer Survival* puts forward that the nonhuman has agency; words typed on a screen, read aloud, or written down are not the only markers of literacy.

For instance, in my story above, the land possesses agency. I argue that the hill and lake my grandfather had built, had asked me to pray away, and had eventually been drained and bulldozed were as much a literacy sponsor as my grandfather. In a model of animate literacies, the *who* of literacy sponsorship expands to include the *what* and *where*. Do I believe I prayed away the mountain? No. My prayers for the mountain, though, were still significant because they taught me how to read and write myself into my grandfather's world. They taught me how my faith was different from my grandfather's, in turn how different my papaw and I were. Another matter here is what is missing. I literally removed myself from dealing with my grandparents because I was beat by my dad for my queerness. Pain and trauma taught me absence, made me literate in ways that others who haven't shared similar grief aren't. I knew what triggered my dad, whether the words I spoke, music I listened to, or my bodily disposition. Every spanking and bruise wrote on my body new ways to navigate and read the world around me.

I'd like to also highlight the dreaming of my grandfather in my narrative that propelled me to act in the waking world around me. Am I suggesting that omens and prophecy are legitimate modes of understanding the world? Perhaps. What matters here isn't the validity of dreams or prognostications but that these literacy practices exist and should be considered significant places to study literacy, if not literacy sponsors altogether. If I didn't interpret my barrage of nightmares as significant agents, I don't know how I'd come to find out my paternal grandfather had passed.

I begin with a story for a couple of reasons. First, my prelude resembles the beginnings of a literacy narrative, a common method and genre of understanding how literacy is obtained by individuals. The Digital Archive of Literacy Narratives, housing over six thousand audio, multimodal, and textual narratives that trace the many ways people become literate, is testament to the diffusion of the literacy narrative as a critical method in the field of writing, rhetoric, and literacy studies.[4] Throughout

Prologue xiii

Reading, Writing, and Queer Survival, I engage with stories, both my own and of five participants, which act as case studies for my analysis. Notice how my story above doesn't focus primarily on texts. In this case, I'm referring to the Bible and the biblical verse that allowed me to understand my relationship with my grandfather. The text is still in my story, yet it's merely shifted from the center of the storytelling, a deviation from typical literacy narratives. This will be true of the participants' storytelling as well. Texts and writing are still in their stories—they are simply not *the* only focus. *Reading, Writing, and Queer Survival* makes this analytic shift to explore what other ways of studying literacy may exist, as well as to seek out which other actors and affects participate in our literacy practices.

I want to be clear that my intention is not to forgo studying text-based literacy. Nor is it my goal to dismiss the years of studying reading and writing in one clean swipe. By shifting focus away from solely writers and readers, writing and reading, I seek to reveal that literacy is caught up in an ongoing, emergent assemblage of various actors. This project adds to the posthumanist frameworks more established in rhetorical theories but still emerging in some literacy theoretical circles, although we need *more* room to explore and reconceptualize literacy for the nonhuman through a new materialist and posthumanist lens.[5] I believe we have a whole world to gain if we panned out the scope of what we study in literacy scholarship.

What would posthumanist literacy look like? How could we apply tenets of new materialism to literacy studies? Candace R. Kuby, Karen Spector, and Jaye Johnson Thiel ask these questions and more in their collection, *Posthumanism and Literacy Education: Knowing/Becoming/Doing Literacies.* They take up the task of engaging how a posthumanist perspective of literacy may begin to take shape: "This book wrestles with the epistemological, ontological, and ethical limitations of [humanisms], and the chapters herein aim to open spaces for the reader to consider the possibilities of posthuman literacies, particularly more-than-just-human, or just Man's, ways of knowing/

becoming/doing literacies.... We too wonder what is left out of the 'field of knowers' in literacy education when we rely solely on humanist orientations to research and pedagogy."[6]

The authors see the value of shifting our emphasis on human-based epistemology because they recognize, as does this project, how literacy involves nonhumans as well. Yet the authors are not apt to remove the human from literacy studies because "we couldn't get rid of the human even if we wanted to, which we don't, as we are always a part of interpreting, writing, and representing literacy research."[7] The authors and I agree, and that's precisely one of the reasons I turn to storytelling and participant-based research. As you will read, I detail further how a new materialist and posthumanist approach can help us in literacy studies in places like Appalachia.

A posthumanist approach, as the authors see it, "questions humanist orientations and assumptions to interpret the ways in which they are problematic."[8] Perhaps, most important to their aims and to my own, the authors see posthumanism as a way to explore literacy differently: "Simply, most theories in literacy education are human centered, even if they discuss materials and texts (nonhumans). The way the human is centered in these dominant theories conceptualizes subjectivity, agency and ways of knowing/becoming/doing in philosophically different ways than posthumanism does."[9]

Kuby, Spector, and Thiel focus on posthumanist approaches in literacy education, whereas, overall, *Reading, Writing, and Queer Survival* aims to showcase how nonhumans have been present in our stories of our literacies and of literacy study all along. I also would add that I treat place as an agential actor, with its own capacity to affect literacy.

I detail in chapter 2 why I choose Appalachia as my site of research but would like to acknowledge up front that I realize the risks that accompany writing about nonhuman and nonprint-based literacy practices in an area that is already stereotyped with being illiterate in the more traditional sense of the term. In no way am I trying to justify the stereotypes of

Appalachians being unable to read and write. Scholars elsewhere have disproven these claims already.[10] While I call attention to nontextual literacies in Appalachia, I do so to show how my participants' reading and writing and other forms of meaning-making have been shaped by a range of actors. It is my amicable goal to show that place—and especially Appalachian places—has an active role to play in our study of literacy if we made even more room for nonhumans in our field and methodologies; it isn't merely where you are reading and writing but how place shapes your reading and writing. In fact, I figure through expanding literacy practices to include nonhumans—to reveal the many configurations that develop through embodied lives with literacy—our definitions, studies, and methodologies of literacy are enriched with possibility, not shut down because of limiting ourselves to text-based or alphabetic literacy practices alone. I am with literacy scholars Leander and Boldt in thinking there is more to literacy than *only* reading and writing, and I'm willing to explore those possibilities with an open mind: "Unless as researchers we begin traveling in the unbounded circles that literacy travels in, we will miss literacy's ability to participate in unruly ways because we only see its properties. We can hold literacy at the center of the world only as long as we keep it in place at the center of our world. What might we make of the invitation to consider literacy in 'and . . . and . . . and . . .' relations?"[11]

I'd like to imagine in what follows as exploring these "and . . . and . . . and" relations in literacy. *Reading, Writing, and Queer Survival* is invested in seeing literacy as relational and takes up Leander and Boldt's question as thinking of literacy outside of our own scholarly bound view of literacy. I hope my reader keeps this in mind as they move through these pages.

A Note on Participants and Data

Following other scholarship of studying literacy by collecting and analyzing "data"—a term I mostly avoid because it rings of sterile, aseptic technique rinsing off any personality—I want to highlight some key information as to how I approach the stories in this book. Know that when I write of *stories*, I am aligning with the conventions of literacy narrative "data" but attempting to imbue life, animating what is often considered inert evidence in academe. Many scholars look to literacy narratives and person-based interviews to study literacy. The same can be said for the acquiring of evidence in *Reading, Writing, and Queer Survival*: I collect queer Appalachian stories and tell my own as the grounds from which a theory of animate literacies can emerge.

I have only two criteria for my participants: (1) They must identify as queer in some way (broadly and personally defined), and I make this explicit through the participation consent form—they might belong to the LGBTQ+ community, embrace nonnormative sex and pleasure, live with a "crip" body.[12] (2) The second criterion links my participants together, underpinning animate literacies' focus on place: Appalachia. They may not necessarily *identify* as Appalachian but must be *from* Appalachia in some way (think: have family from Appalachia, moved to or away from Appalachia, been born in Appalachia but don't live there, etc.). I leave how they qualify their relationship to Appalachia up to my participants. It should also be stated my participants are all at least eighteen years old. Some participants did not share their age but merely confirmed they were of consenting age.

The participants were recruited among acquaintances in Appalachia, through colleagues, and through word of mouth in my personal life. Some participants were recruited through the community Facebook sites to which I belong such as Queer PhD Network and the Conference on College Composition and Communication's Queer Caucus and Appalachian Special Interest Group—I also shared a call for participation on my own Facebook profile and asked friends to share. It is important to note that some participants are people I have never met except through the venues I outline here, while others are close friends, even family. Grabill's articulation of research stance—"understood as a position or a set of beliefs and obligations that show how one acts a researcher"—is critical to maintain levels of openness not only with my participants but also with my readers.[13] My relationship to my readers and to the Appalachian queers who contribute to my research is based on transparency. There are five stories. Justin's story is the focus of chapter 3. Lexi, Elizabeth, Lara, and Macy are the focal points of chapter 4. I met Justin through a friend in 2015. Lexi was recruited to participate in my research through a mutual friend. Elizabeth, Lara, and Macy reached out via email after my call for participants was issued on Facebook.

I use a set of interview questions (see appendix) in order to engage four areas in my participants' lives: *trauma* (whatever this means to them), their understanding of and their relationship to their *bodies*, the role *place* and land play in their lives, and their *spiritual beliefs* and practices. These four categories shift away from human-linguistic privileging in current scholarship. The four categories help in exploring how affects—especially those associated with trauma and spirituality—have agency in my participants' lives. The same with the other two categories, bodies and places, but pertaining to the world of matter—the nonhuman, objects, matterings.

I want to note here that I embrace the fluid nature of queerness in such a way to allow for conversations and disruptions to occur during the interview process. Queer person–based research is messy, and I embrace the possibility that a structured interview may not always be able to represent the polyvalent nature of how literacies function in my participants' lives.[14] The interview questions, then, were merely a departure point to enable the storytelling. Because the interview process requires textual transcription, I used audio recording through my iPhone and audio recorder. Participants' real names are not used unless they requested otherwise, and even then, I don't reveal if their aliases are real or not. More of an academic audience will realize that I don't use coding to organize my data. Instead, I listened to the interviews on repeat for hours, searching for metaphors that animated their stories of literacy. Metaphor is a critical analytic that I use and expound on in my methodology chapter.

The interviews each were at least an hour long with some nearing 120 minutes. The result was over 20,000 words of storytelling. Because animate literacies search for the agency of places, things, and how both can linger via affect, I ran key moments of the stories through a word cloud generator, such as wordclouds.com. I recall a key researcher in the field of composition and rhetoric studies doing this once at a preeminent academic conference.[15] It visually renders the words in a text—an interview, an essay, a chapter, and so forth—as a cluster of terms. The larger the word, the more frequently it was used. I didn't include these word clouds here because that was part of the writing process for me as a listener of these stories. Justin's story showcased water heaters, the focal point of chapter 3 and his story. Lexi's story, run through the generator, illustrated that her dad and drugs had a role to play in the way she used words to feel through her lived world. Bisexuality was shown large and central to Elizabeth's storytelling, while Macy's narrative showcased the relationship with her boyfriend. Laura's use of the word *condom* stood out, designating my analytical focus. This isn't a typified means of studying literacy.

Another element here that I attempt as a researcher is to make myself seen inside the research process; I'm not separate from the data here. I listened to these stories; my notes, the traveling through Appalachia, the relationships I have to these stories are intimately woven into the methodologies that animate literacies propose. That's why I weave story everywhere: at the beginning with my papaw's hillside; as a means to explore how we have storied Appalachia as a queer place in America, one that demands queer methodologies to study; listening to queer Appalachians' stories and their literacies; and finally, how a theory of animate literacies reveals that, as pedagogues, we can use our stories to animate our teaching when we are far from the places that made us.

The Structure of Reading, Writing, and Queer Survival

Reading, Writing, and Queer Survival intersects with a number of scholarly pursuits: This is a literacy project, one that seeks to emphasize posthuman elements, providing an example of how to do literacy studies research with a posthumanist bent, and, in doing so, reveals the importance of place-centered approaches to literacy; Because place is important to Appalachia and Appalachian studies, *Reading, Writing, and Queer Survival* provides its readers with a nuanced exploration of literacies for queer Appalachians.

To accomplish the first, it's important that I provide my reader with an exploration of literacy studies, its history, and its sometimes overemphasis on human-only theories, as well as how literacy sponsorship has been a primary method of ascertaining the literacy an individual possesses and acquires. I recognize that literacy sponsorship isn't *the* only metric and method to study literacy; it has been frequented as a tool to do so, nevertheless. Because my reader may not have picked up this book for its contribution to literacy studies alone, it's critical that I provide context and history. Next, in chapter 1, you'll find a brief history of literacy studies, which leads to an alternative definition of animate literacies. My goal is to expose some of the ways American literacy studies—I am focusing on American literacy studies because Appalachia is my site of research, a region critical to American history—have often narrowly focused on the human domain in its treatment of literacy. You're not going to get much of Appalachia until chapter 2 because I must initially provide some academic context. As I'll show, place takes on greater significance with animate literacies, in terms of both where we study literacy and how we theorize its goal in treating place as actively participating in its study.

There is another theoretical element here that needs clarification: queer, which is intimately tethered to Appalachia. Chapter 2 explores in more complicated ways how my approach to literacy examines the queer. But more generally, I deploy the word because of my positionality as a researcher and the identities of my Appalachian participants. Queerness has come to the fore in Appalachian studies in recent years, with research and writing of/on/with/by queer Appalachians proliferating. *Reading, Writing, and Queer Survival* is in conversation with other works such as the now-canonical *Storytelling in Queer Appalachia*, which placed queerness and Appalachia next to one another for the first time in such public ways in American discourse. Neema Avashia's memoir, *Another Appalachia*, comes to mind, for it is her own exploration of place-based literacies in West Virginia. The 2019 collection of *LGBTQ Fiction and Poetry from Appalachia* (edited by Jeff Mann and Julia Watts) is another hub of voices, of queer literacies, that emerge from the places in Appalachia. Personally, as my prologue shows, I've known that queerness operates in different ways in Appalachia. I've witnessed how Appalachian queerness complicates the literacies in the region. Literacy was a matter of survival in my upbringing. Queerness shaped my literacy; literacy shaped my queerness. It was abundantly obvious for me that queerness and literacy, even queer literacy, were different when I left the Kentucky knobs to live in more midwestern, northern, and/or metropolitan regions of our country. Over my lifelong pursuit of studying words, language, reading, and writing, I had questions that bore my theory of *Reading, Writing, and Queer Survival*. So when I use the word *queer*, when *queer* is used in this text, it is referring in its most basic utilization (if such an aspect of queerness can even exist) that queer individuals experience the world outside of cishet frameworks of desire, of embodiment, of living and surviving, of meaning-making, of reading and writing.

Queerness also informs my treatment of Appalachia as a research site in chapter 2. Appalachian scholars agree that Appalachia is a queer place because of its otherization, adding a layer of complexity to queerness in *Reading, Writing, and Queer Survival*. In this chapter, I detail my methodologies of collecting queering stories as a means of analyzing animate literacies' focus on *being with*, or relationality. I suggest that queer metaphors give us insight into the constellations of actants that comprise animate literacies. I conclude this chapter with a new analytic: *metaphoric tracking*, a method of listening and searching for metaphors in queer storytelling. It shifts the methodological questions of literacy studies from *Who taught us to read and write?* and *What or how do we read and write?* to a question of *How do we use literacy to read and write the world around us?* There are two forms of metaphor tracking that I'm interested in: literacy matters and literacy affects.

Chapter 3, "Matters of the Closet," takes up the former mode of metaphoric tracking, using the metaphor of coming out of the closet to illustrate how nonhumans can have agency in queer storytelling. I take the closet to be a literal actor in the literacy practice of coming-out narratives. I spend time with a single story that belongs to Justin, an Appalachian from southeastern Ohio. I theorize Justin's closet as being full of human and non-human literacy sponsors that dissuade and enable his coming out. I think through Justin's story as an example of how metaphors are representative of our relationship with the world and how they expose how being with others is central to a theory of animate literacies. "Queer Affinities," chapter 4, reveals how literacies with their multitudinous practices have lasting effects that linger past reading and writing. In other words, this chapter explores how affinities with and for others form through literacy practices and can affect us even after reading and writing is over. This chapter also deals with literacy in a more traditional manner. I begin with writing, reading, and other literacy practices of four participants, Lexi, Elizabeth, Macy, and Lara, all of whom are from various parts of Appalachia. I then engage with their stories and how their literacy affects linger past more conventional models of studying literacies.

To close, in "Carrying the Mountains to the Sea," I story a pedagogy of animate literacies. Detailing my journey from the Kentucky knobs to the shores of Cape Cod, I offer a praxis of animate literacies in my own classroom. Designing a course around Appalachian cultures at Massachusetts Maritime Academy, I weave together the affective realities of being an Appalachian expat writing, reading, teaching, quite literally, on the Atlantic coastline. It may seem like a deviation from person-based research, perhaps perceived as a way to shift away from the stories I collect in chapters 3 and 4. I'd argue this is in fact the opposite: this chapter is an extension of what Justin, Lexi, Elizabeth, Macy, and Lara taught me. Their animate literacies helped shape how my own queer Appalachian literacies move, how all literacies are movable across places and land. By writing with the research participants' stories, I was changed as an academic. So I end with a praxis chapter on how we can take home, place, and identity and move through this queer world.

1

Animacy, Literacy, and Queer Agency

Animacy as a linguistic construct deals with the liveliness or sentience of words (nouns most often) and how language, grammar, and meaning are constructed in hierarchies of agency.[1] In these animacy hierarchies, using the English language as an example, humans have more agency than, let's say, an animal. The animal is imbued with more agency than perhaps a plant. A plant more so than a mineral. For this reason, we wouldn't say *The ball throws the child*. Instead, *The child throws the ball*. The ball, in this sentence, doesn't have equal agency of a child. Ad infinitum, animacy organizes agency.

Mel Chen's *Animacies: Biopolitics, Racial Mattering, and Queer Affect* works to decenter and disrupt animacy hierarchies, where Chen questions the hierarchization of language and meaning, demonstrating how common orderings spill over, fail, and even leak.[2] Chen "draws upon recent debates about sexuality, race, environment, and affect to consider how matter that is considered insensate, immobile, deathly or otherwise 'wrong' animates cultural life in important ways."[3] The linguistic term *animacy*, Chen notes, isn't considered a word by conventional dictionaries, while the related word *animate* is: "Having the following Latin etymology: 'ad. L. *animātus* filled with life, *also*, disposed, inclined, f. *animāre* to breathe, to quicken; f. *anima* air, breath, life, soul, mind'. . . . *Animus*, on the other hand, derives from the Latin, meaning '(1) soul, (2) mind, (3) mental impulse, disposition, passion,' and is defined as 'actuating feeling, disposition in a particular direction, animating spirit or temper, usually of a hostile character; hence, animosity.'"[4]

Chen argues that "animacy is much more than the state of being animate, and it is precisely the absence of a consensus around its meaning that leaves it open to both inquiry and resignification" and digs "into animacy as a specific kind of affective and material construct that is not only nonneutral in relation to animals, humans, and living and dead things, but is shaped by race and sexuality, mapping various biopolitical realizations of animacy in the contemporary culture of the United States."[5] Extending Chen's work, this project turns its focus away from biopolitics and looks instead to more immediate ways affective and material conditions of literacy reveal that literacy is, like animacies, nonneutral. In order to animate literacy, we need to broaden the importance of the affective and material dimensions of literacy.

It is precisely these binaries of the animate and inanimate, the living and dead, that propel Chen's argument: "[Animacy] seeks to trouble this binary of life and nonlife as it offers a different way to conceive of relationality and intersubjective exchange."[6] If applied to literacy, animacies may cause us to reconsider what it means to be literate in terms of relationality and interbeing with the nonhuman. Perhaps most importantly, Chen's animacies' flexible, fluid, not-yet-alive but not-yet-dead nature relies on queerness and queer theory: Chen's sense of "'queer' refers, as might be expected, to challenges to the conventional order of sex, reproduction, and intimacy, though it at times also refers to animacy's veering-away from dominant ontologies and the normativities they promulgate."[7] Similarly, it could be said my theorizing of animate literacies relies on queer literacies through which to rethink how we are intimate with the world around us.

Chen's work on animacies does not focus "on the politics of a monolithic *queer*," such as the institutionalized "Queer" of Queer Studies, but instead on its linguistic qualities and possibilities.[8] As if to save *queer* from the solidified meaning it's beginning to gain in academe, Chen examines "the politics of *polyvalence* that are instituted in part by the 'bleeding' of *queer* into diffuse parts of speech."[9] My project takes a similar approach to queer, queerness, and queers. When I use the word *queer*, I am drawing from a conglomeration of queer scholars next to the lived experiences of both myself and those of whom I interview in later chapters.[10] I take queer/ing to be disruptive, disorienting, wrought with failures—embracing mess, the profane, and the ugly, all the while knowing that queering can undo selfhood and imagine possibilities not yet actualized.[11] At some level, I'd say, I never truly lose sight of queer's initial relationship with desire, sex as act, and bodies that are nonnormative, all factors that are woven throughout this project.

Because this project is about literacy, Chen's queering of animacy theory acts as a parallel with my intentions of adding to literacy scholarship that explores queerness. By borrowing from the *Animacies* framework, I hope to honor Chen's influence in linguistic and queer theory and carry over their work into the field of literacy. Chen takes "a rather uncommon linguistic approach of studying" the failings of the conceptual dominant hierarchy of animacy.[12] I ask: What are the dominant concepts of literacy and its study? Furthermore, how do our understandings and studying of literacy work to reinscribe its own hierarchies? *Reading, Writing, and Queer Survival* draws on Chen's theory of animacies to ask these questions and more, proposing we rethink humancentric models of literacy.

Chen's ideas of literacy inform much of the following pages; however, before I can arrive at a theory of animate literacies, I must first consider the past of literacy studies. This introduction will offer a brief scholarly history of literacy studies, beginning in the 1960s and ending with more current research with a focus on critiquing the anthropocentric elements of the social turn and theories of literacy sponsorship in the field. By engaging with new materialist thought and posthumanist principles, this introduction concludes by making an offer to its readers to entertain a new definition of literacy at its end, proffering literacy as an energetic exchange rather than only an ability or a resource.[13]

Finding Literacy

Oftentimes, I believe when we talk about literacy, we take for granted its meaning. What exactly is literacy? How can we define it? And if literacy proves difficult to define, how, then, can we study it? It could be said that literacy is colloquially understood to be the ability to read and write. Looking around my desk, I see notes I've taken, written as reminders to myself; birthday cards from friends; my daily affirmations; and I write to you, my dear reader, under the presupposition that you can extrapolate meaning from the words I type here. Both the reader and the writer, at least to some degree, function under the pretense of being literate, of possessing literacy. Even *Merriam-Webster* tautologically defines *literacy* as "the quality or state of being literate," wherein *literate* has two definitions: "(a) educated, cultured; (b) able to read and write" and "(a) versed in literature or creative writing: literary; (b) lucid, polished; (c) having knowledge or competence."[14]

Literacy is at the same time easy to understand as the ability to read and write but then complicated enough to have various definitions, such as the one above. I'm not satisfied with literacy being narrowly defined as an ability to write and read alone.

Certainly, literacy involves words. But literacy is much more, as Jacqueline Royster argues. Engaging with the comments of Sojourner Truth to argue for literacy as "emanating from lived experience," Royster rethinks the term: "Literacy is a sociocultural phenomenon, a use of language, a component of a complex system of understanding and intents from which decoding and encoding text must inevitably get their shape, direction, and momentum."[15] Language. Understanding. Decoding and encoding. These words in particular stand out in Royster's passage above. Continuing on, she spells out that literacy is "a sociocognitive ability," an ability to "identify, think through, refine, and solve problems."[16] By using the compound *sociocognitive*, she intends to highlight literacy as including "ways of knowing and believing" as well as "ways of doing," pressing the "boundaries between orality and literacy to be questioned from an even broader range of language practices."[17] Royster's framing of literacy gets us closer to the literacy I am using herein. Animate literacies, however, will complicate two elements of Royster's literacy: the framing of literacy as a cognitive ability and the focus on solely human exchange (i.e., the *socio* of *sociocognitive*).

Royster's definition sets up my project by revealing that there are many ways to be literate. Perhaps most importantly, though, her expansion of literacy as a social praxis is a telling marker of a historic shift in literacy studies. Prior to the 1960s, literacy was usually theorized in terms of autonomy. Literacy was "independent of social context, an autonomous variable."[18] The individual was responsible for their own literacy; society, culture, and/or ideology supposedly had no influence or role to play. This later came to be named the "literacy myth," which assumes that literacy is key to a progressive, "modern" society. Literacy became a primary catalyst for the invention of the modern subject; in other words, literacy has an intimate relationship with the modern era, where "literacy, then, as a measure of modernity, on either the individual or the societal level, becomes a symbol—and just as its benefits are located in the areas of abstraction and symbolism, so are its functions."[19]

The urgency of literacy's social impact came to be understood to stratify socioeconomic class, with scholars pointing out that this was "a system of ownership built on the ownership of literacy," where "to be literate is to be legitimate."[20] Literacy is viewed as a social technology that recognizes literate subjects as legitimate. This observation has been made, too, but in terms of colonization, where "writing came into the picture when the consolidation of vernacular languages . . . needed the letter to tame the voice and grammar to control the mobility of the flow of speech. Writing was the end result of an evolutionary process, one of the highest achievements of human intelligence."[21] Literacy, then, is also always linked to ideology. Literacy isn't inert or an unadulterated tool that an individual possesses. Literacy is complex, social, and wrought with power.

Because of these reasons, scholars have defined literacy in several ways. One famous definition comes from Deborah Brandt, where literacy is treated as a resource, especially insofar as having economic value. She puts it plainly: "Literacy is a resource in the way that electricity is a resource: Its circulation keeps lights on. Literacy is also a productive resource, a means of production and reproduction, including a means by which legacies of human experience move from past to future and by which, for many, identities are made and sustained."[22]

Brandt shows us that literacy certainly does have economic value, and it's an economically stratifying resource to boot. The idea that literacy is a resource, skill, and tool with economic capital is prevalent throughout the entirety of Brandt's argument. It's my aim in this project to illustrate how literacy not only drives social and economic systems in our lives but also animates us on the most physical and affective levels of our embodied experiences.

Animating Literacy Sponsorship

Deborah Brandt's legacy arguably began back in 1998, when she initially advanced the concept of literacy sponsor in her article "Sponsors of Literacy." Recall that literacy sponsors are "any agents, local or distant, concrete or abstract, who enable, support, teach, model, as well as recruit, regulate, suppress, or withhold literacy—and gain advantage of it in some way."[23]

Literacy sponsorship gained more traction in her publication of *Literacy in American Lives*, wherein she uses literacy sponsorship as her primary analytic tool. Brandt's article has been cited over 460 times, while *Literacy in American Lives* has been referenced over 1,000 times, according to Google Scholar—a result, I believe, that is in part due to her coining of *literacy sponsorship*.[24] Literacy sponsorship, whenever engaged, is always linked to the human, whether the sponsor is an individual, an organization, or a larger institution such as government agencies, churches / religious groups, or schools.[25] I recognize that literacy sponsorship isn't *the* defining tool of literacy studies. An examination of sponsorship does reveal nonetheless that literacy studies can easily disregard the nonhuman, especially in American scholarly circles.

I realize that one can read Brandt's articulation that sponsors could be "concrete or abstract" as making space for the inclusion I'm calling for here. Yet I do not believe that Brandt intended an "abstract" agent could include objects or affects due to her last condition of said agent gaining advantage of extending literacy to another subject. For example, if I am arguing that affects can have agency—an argument central to animacies theory—and even be thought of as literacy sponsors, we must consider how affects can sometimes fail or serve no purpose and thus cannot gain any sort of advantage.

In fact, Brandt makes it clear that when she speaks of literacy sponsors, she is discussing individuals who "set the terms for access to literacy and wield powerful incentives for compliance and loyalty."[26] Sponsors help explain "a range of human relationships and ideological pressures that turn up at the scenes of literacy learning," and while she mentions that sponsorship "is a concept useful for tracking literacy's material" aspects, the material is always a result of the literacy sponsor imparting literacy in some way.[27] She gives the instance of office documents that may result from a literacy sponsor sponsoring an individual: when someone applies for a loan, for instance, the loan officer has the sponsored individual sign a contract, hold a pen, use a desk, and so on. My point, though, is that for Brandt, the material is never the source of literacy, only its result.

In my research, I've failed to uncover many scholars who fully question the humancentric nature of literacy sponsors in Brandt's definition. It's a given in most work in literacy studies that an agent is a human or a group of humans under the guise of an organization or institution.[28] Among my search for scholars who extend Brandt's concept of sponsorship, some more interesting findings include Lisa Mastrangelo's argument that community cookbooks act as literacy sponsors, representing the communities that write them; Galbreath's exploration of how food literacy is sponsored by land-grant universities, their extension services to local communities, and the 4-H; Trace's suggestion that boys' and girls' agricultural clubs are sponsors of the early American twentieth-century Progressive Era; and Cook and Ryle's suggestion that comic book superheroes are acting as literacy sponsors.[29]

Scholars are already seeking to expand and complicate literacy sponsorship. Two examples stand out. First, acknowledging that sponsorship "is a messy process," Sara Webb-Sunderhaus posits that "contradictory messages about literacy could come from the same person, such that the same person could be both a sponsor and an inhibitor."[30] In other words, agents can either foster literacy or inhibit it and even at times do both. The second example comes from Kara Poe Alexander, who argues that an individual can function "both as sponsor and sponsored," arriving at the conclusion that sponsorship can be reciprocal.[31] Others have pointed out that genres can be literacy sponsors.[32] The understanding that literacy sponsorship doesn't have to work in only one direction shows that sponsorship is more complex than the original definition offers. I'd like to think *Reading, Writing, and Queer Survival* can show that sponsorship can work between nonhumans and humans as well.

Along these lines, Brandt (in a later article with Clinton) explored this idea of moving away from human-only agents of literacy sponsorship. Brandt and Clinton attempt to "show what new questions can be asked and perspectives gleaned once the door between people and things is opened, and things are given the status of social actors."[33] The authors engage Latour in order "to dissolve [dichotomies of global and local] by treating literacy not as an outcome or accomplishment of local practices but as a participant in them, as an actor or what Latour coins an 'actant' in its own right. Literacy is neither a deterministic force nor a creation of local agents. Rather it participates in social practices in the form of objects and technologies, whose meanings are not usually created nor exhausted by the locales in which they are taken up."[34]

I agree with Brandt and Clinton's use of Latour's idea that objects "are active mediators—imbuing, resisting, recrafting" within literacy.[35] Animate literacies attempt to pick up where Brandt and Clinton leave off in their essay. Animate literacies agree with Brandt and Clinton that "figuring out what things are doing with people in a setting becomes as important as figuring out what people are doing with things in a setting."[36] I'd like to add that we must approach matter and objects on their own terms, and paying attention to affects, places, and other nonhuman agents in queer storytelling is crucial. More importantly, a theory of animate literacies treats the *force* of affect as a site of literacy.[37]

The many examples of sponsorship that I pointed to above place either the person or the text or both central as literacy sponsor. Animate literacies are deeply concerned with the lasting effects of the literacy sponsor. Where Brandt sees literacy sponsors as agents who influence literacy in a number of ways, I urge us to complicate agents of literacy sponsorship to include the *what* and *where*. The boundaries of literacies should not stop at who affects the literacy in our lives but become porous, complicating the relationships between material and affective dimensions in the many places we find ourselves. In several ways, I see an expansion of literacy sponsorship addresses the point that Kuby, Spector, and Thiel make explicit in *Posthumanism and Literacy Education* for why we need a new materialist and posthuman approach to literacy studies: "We need theories to think with that don't try to isolate, extract, desiccate, and ossify according [to] the logics of neoliberalism and late capitalism, which will, we believe, not stop until there is no vitality left to extract. We need an ethics of interdisciplinary, interspecies doings at the heart of our work with student/materials, always seen as immersed with complex interconnections that fan out."[38] Animating literacy sponsorship, to understand that literacy involves a web of actors, is one step that can be taken to build such ethics.

Animate Literacies' Queer Agents

Ultimately, an ongoing premise of my project argues that by examining overlooked or underacknowledged agents of literacy for queers (e.g., recall the mountain in my prologue), we can develop a richer understanding of particular places, matter, and affects. I use the terms *agents* and *actors* interchangeably, mainly as a stylistic choice but also because actors have agency, which means they can be considered agencies, or agents. Many new materialist thinkers and posthumanists make a similar stylistic choice in the interchangeability between these terms.[39]

If literacy sponsors are agents, it follows that they have the capacity for agency. Then literacy scholars, it goes without stating, accept agency as an integral part of literacy and have for some time now. Agency is "understood as our capacity to act or to affect others and be affected."[40] It denotes how we do things.[41] Notably, Cooper has argued that agency is embodied and emergent and "based in individuals' lived knowledge that their actions are their own."[42] In the case of democratic rhetorics, Arabella Lyon theorizes at length how agency can be understood as the "navigation, maintenance, and construction of useful norms as well as resistance and subordination" of such norms.[43] Agency and queerness have been linked a number of times too.[44] More recently, Pritchard highlights in their work with Black LGBTQ+ people's literacies that literacy agency is made up from "uses of literacy" by individuals and institutions.[45] In short, literacy scholars often tether agency to the individual—agency belongs to the literate subject.

Freire and Macedo may offer a minute deviation from this position but nonetheless never fully shift perspectives. In their discussion on the role of individualism, society, and literacy, Freire makes this claim about human agency: "It could appear that a position that is profoundly individualistic would end up stimulating and respecting the role of the human agency. In truth, it denies all dimensions of human agency. Why does the individualistic position end up working against the real role of human agency? Because the only real subjectivity is that which confronts its contradictory relationship to objectivity.... Human agency makes sense and flourishes only when subjectivity is understood in it dialectical, contradictory, dynamic relationship objectivity, from which it derives."[46]

By proxy of this dialogic relationship, the authors infamously argue, "Reading the world always precedes reading the word, and reading the word implies continually reading the world."[47] I acquiesce to such a view of literacy; the world can be legible, and our interaction with it enables us to become literate—not once and for all but through an ongoing interaction with it. Although, still, this doesn't imbue the world with any more agency that it had before. That is to say, I am still the one reading the world. The onus of individual human agency has simply shifted from conventional texts to a rendering of the world as text. Freire's expansion of literacy to include the world as a text opens a conversation, though, on how we may consider the impact of nonhuman actors in our theories and methodologies. I'd like to add to Freire's position, asking not *How do we read the world*? but *How may the world read and write us*? In other words, what would happen if we considered nonhuman actors equally as animate as we are?

I find recent scholarship on visual rhetoric and circulation theories by Laurie Gries to be useful in terms of making sense of agents and agency. In attempts to call for a new materialist rhetorical approach, Gries defines agency as "an act of intervention," where it is "not some capacity that any single image has and carries with it just as it is not some capacity that any single person has."[48] Admittedly, Gries is making a new materialist intervention to theories of rhetoric and not literacy. However, her denoting agency as both an act and an intervention, which no single person can possess, begins to expand literacy past agents that have something to gain from sponsoring literacy.

One way the queering of agency here begins to take shape is to refigure the agents of literacy sponsorship as queer. In *Queer Phenomenology*, Sara Ahmed offers insights that are helpful in coming to grips with how queerness blurs boundaries between queers and queer nonhuman agents. Ahmed, by way of Merleau-Ponty, argues that bodies extend into space in relation to objects they are directed toward.[49] Yet when those bodies are oriented in ways that aren't apparent, or "straight," they are to be understood as queer: since queer "is, after all, a spatial term, which then gets translated into a sexual term, a term for a twisted sexuality that does not follow a 'straight line,' a sexuality that is bent and crooked."[50] While her talk of lines, orientations, and phenomenology offers rich critiques of space and bodies, I bring her into this conversation on animate literacies to complicate a queer approach to agency. Ahmed notes agency as "a matter . . . of how bodies come into contact with objects, as a contact that is never simply between two entities . . . as each entity is already shaped by contact with others."[51] Carried over into literacy sponsorship, we could say that the very dyad of the sponsor and sponsored is an idealistic construct from its inception then, not one based in reality generally speaking but especially for queers. Behind each agent is a complex web of agential relations that cannot easily be reduced to a single sponsor or set of sponsors; agency cannot be drawn in a direct line.

Furthermore, what happens when such agents fail or don't support literacy in the ways they're intended to? What if they don't follow the straight path from sponsor to sponsored? Failure has long been thought of as queer. Halberstam has made this point very clear: "Under certain circumstances failing, losing, forgetting, unmaking, undoing, unbecoming, not knowing may in fact offer more creative, more cooperative, more surprising ways of being in the world. Failing is something queers do and have always done exceptionally well."[52]

To be queer and to queer both invoke a sense of failure, and the same should be considered when we discuss agency. Hearkening back to the notion of compulsory heterosexuality, queerness also fails to reproduce straightness.[53] That is to ask: What happens when a queer resists the literacy supposedly sponsored? Resisting literacy reproduction appears to become, in a sense, queer. My point is that queer agency can invert the hierarchies of the inappropriate, the material, the nonhuman in order to create new meaning. Queerness via animacies is "an operator that shiftily [navigates] gradations of matter, including things, actions, and sensibilities."[54] In relation to literacy, then, we must let go of sponsorship that clings desperately to the human at its apex and turn instead to consider how queer agents can reshape literacy altogether. I'd like to make one last turn: If *Reading, Writing, and Queer Survival* arrives at literacy through queer agency, what do we then make of literacy?

Animating Literacy

Literacy scholarship has explored how literacy is bound to subjectivity and citizenship; involves disciplining power of the individual; is tied to ideologies, culture, and societal practices; can be unique to place; can stratify along many social categories including but not limited to race and gender; and can entail literacy events in which orality and literacy intersect. But what is literacy? Let's entertain James Paul Gee's definition of literacy as "the mastery of or fluent control over a secondary Discourse" for a moment. Belonging to the New Literacy Studies movement, Gee was among the first to theoretically *define* literacy as separate from writing and reading alone but as a social practice, which he theorizes as Discourse:

> At any moment we are using language we must say or write the right thing in the right way while playing the right social role and (appearing) to hold the right values, beliefs, and attitudes. Thus, what is important is not language, and surely not grammar, but *saying (writing)-doing-being-valuing-believing combinations.* These combinations I call "Discourses," with a capital "D" ("discourse" with a little "d," to me, means connected stretches of language that make sense, so "discourse" is part of "Discourse"). Discourse are ways of being in the world; they are forms of life which integrate words, acts, values, beliefs, attitudes, and social identities as well as gestures, glances, body positions, and clothes.[55]

Gee draws the distinction between primary Discourses and secondary Discourses. The initial or primary Discourse is "the one we first use to make sense of the world and interact with others," our "primary socializing group."[56] This initial Discourse carries us into other secondary Discourses throughout our lives.[57] Secondary Discourses can come in either the dominant or nondominant varieties, with the prior enabling the acquisition of goods, while the latter, nondominant Discourses, "brings solidarity with a particular social network."[58] It is once Gee finds his way through this discursive lexical experiment that he comes to define literacy as being fluent or adept at a secondary Discourse.

Gesturing back to Royster's framing of literacy as involving language as a doing, Gee here also points out that literacy is about language in action. Literacy for Gee deals with ontologies—literacy is about ways of doing and being, if only, albeit, within his framing of Discourses. Let's be careful here, though. Discourse and ontology can be, I realize, at odds with one another. The way we talk about reality and the semantics we use are not always compatible with living in that reality. I'm not sure that Gee would use the word *ontological*, but as

I see it, he does emphasize ontological aspects of literacy in his definition of Discourse.

This shift to literacy as a *doing* indicates an added emphasis that literacy is about the practice of language in both writing and reading and beyond. Take notice that for Gee, the social hasn't been eliminated from literacy. Instead, the social is augmented, at least in his capital-D Discourse. Language alone isn't indicative of literacy because literacy is much more than language. If literacy equals a mastery of a secondary Discourse, then language is only but one component of literacy. Literacy involves acting in social arenas in certain ways ("playing the right social role"), what we say, how we act, our value systems ("words, acts, values, beliefs, attitudes"), even how we position our bodies ("gestures, glances, body positions, and clothes").[59]

Gee has been critiqued for this Discourse/discourse, primary/secondary formula. I'm thinking of Wallace and Alexander's counterarguments about how Gee's work deadens queer rhetorical agency.[60] The authors resist Gee's suggestion that literacy can be acquired via secondary discourses so easily because it presents "a failure to account for sexual identity" and creates "theoretical and critical blind spots" in the "conceptualization of literacy and agency."[61] Gee's assumption that the primary discourse is "a place of safety and/or coherent identity is particularly difficult for queers who may not even have a visibly acknowledged position from which to articulate themselves," and, furthermore, secondary discourses don't always enable queers to have agency in their predominant Discourse.[62] "Put most simply," Alexander and Wallace write, "our concern about the underlying notion of agency in New Literacy Studies [to which Gee belongs] is that it posits an understanding of agency that oversimplifies the relationship between identity and dominant ideologies."[63] I'm in agreement with Alexander and Wallace: literacy rests in part on the propagation of heteronormativity, which queer agency works to actively resist. Their critique is important to note because it makes clear that literacy cannot be as simple as Gee purports, especially for queers and queerness. Yet the authors' engagement with Gee is different than mine. Where they challenge Gee to retheorize queer agency, I look to bring into relief the doingness of Gee's literacy—a point that is, indeed, queer as far as how literacy has been studied and defined up until this point.

What's important—and I cannot stress this enough—from Gee's definition is its ontological perspective: literacy is bound to being. Gee's focus on ways of being, the list gerunds he notes above, is a critical addition that animate literacies rely on and hopefully expand. I worry that this ontological perspective relies too heavily on literacy as existing between people and doesn't lend much in the way of exploring other ontologies. What would happen to literacy if the human wasn't central to literacy's definition? I'm not calling for a complete paradigm shift where literacy exists a priori to humanity or outside of society altogether. It's obvious, I recognize, that literacy is tethered to human interaction. What I am suggesting, however, is when we no longer confine ourselves by thinking that literacy lies only between humans, we can come to terms that literacy as an object of study has mostly ignored the world of matter, animality, organic life, and otherwise—that which isn't human has yet to be acknowledged in literacy. Literacy involves the human, yes, but shouldn't be limited to just us.

I follow Stacey Waite's understanding of literacy being bound to notions of thinkability.[64] According to Waite, literacy involves possibility, what can be imagined and what cannot. Waite, in many ways, picks up where Jonathan Alexander left off in *Literacy, Sexuality, Pedagogy*.[65] For his intervention to include sex and sexuality as a "crucial component of any literacy education," Alexander defines sexual literacy as "the knowledge complex that recognizes the significance of sexuality to self- and communal definition and that critically engages the stories we tell about sex and sexuality to probe them for controlling values and for ways to resist, when necessary, constraining norms."[66] Building on Alexander's use of sexual literacy, Waite points out "that what is thinkable, or imaginable, is part of the process of reading and writing," and thus, I argue, animate literacies should be equally concerned with what's thinkable or imaginable.[67] Much like Royster, Waite suggests that literacy is about process—that when you are writing, you are simultaneously offering a reading to an assumed audience as well as performing a reading in the writing. Reading and writing, coding and decoding are interactional. The doing is a process and an exchange.

Elsewhere, Waite highlights that literacy "means that more must become thinkable, readable—including the idea that what is unthinkable is not there."[68] Other scholars have broken down reading and writing in similar ways to broaden their meaning—where reading "refers to the ability to gather and process knowledge from a variety of 'texts,'" and writing can mean "the ability to transform knowledge to achieve a particular purpose."[69]

Waite's definition doesn't put us completely back at square one, however, where literacy is *only* the act of reading and the act of writing. Waite's literacy is still ontologically tethered to the process of literacy, where to *do literacy* is a way of being. Put another way:

> It is common practice to think of literacy as resulting in a gaining of knowledge or forming new knowledge, but we must also consider the possibility . . . that being literate in gendered cultural norms . . . means learning how to *not know*, how to *not ask*. Or put another way, it means to practice a literacy that precludes other possibilities for knowing and being. . . . It's that the literacy practices we have learned (however invisibility) which it comes to our bodies, when it comes to identity and gender and sex, are practices of *not knowing*, practices where to know *means* quite literally *to not notice, to accept without question the conditions* given to us, the conditions of our very possibility.[70]

Waite articulates how social contractions of gender identity, sex, and sexuality are literacy forces that can exclude possibility.

Later on, Waite points out that queer literacy, then, "involves understanding literacy as bound to seeing and articulating possibility, even when there seems little room to do so."[71] What Waite offers with regard to literacy being concerned with possibility points *Reading, Writing, and Queer Survival* in a productive direction. If we free ourselves from the shackles that literacy works only one way, we can begin engaging with the immediate world around us in new ways too. Our relationships with the land, animals, the air, and objects all take on new meaning when we entertain the queer notion that we can listen to and "read" the world in ways that aren't limited to text.

Reading, Writing, and Queer Survival concerns itself with what is possible with literacy. Which practices in our study of literacy have excluded possible worldviews and actors? What have we not noticed or accepted without questioning the conditions given to us about literacy itself? Much like Waite, I, too, think the way to get closer to these questions—indeed, to even engage with them in the first place—is queer. If queer literacy is about what is possible, then *Reading, Writing, and Queer Survival* has connections to queerness. As such, I'd like to offer a working definition that explains how animate literacies treat literacy herein: literacy is an exchange of forces, emanating from a combination of sign systems, performances, and the sensate, which flow between human and nonhuman agents, in and through particular places, in order to effect change, creating new ways of being with and meaning-making.

My definition of literacy here resists quite a bit in terms of traditional literacy milieu. First, keeping faith that literacy is a process, I define literacy in terms of both an exchange and of having a forcefulness, an energy. Literacy here isn't (only) an ability. Literacy has a life of its own, in other words—although, certainly, I acknowledge that literacy can include abilities, being able, and/or possessing a capability.

As I am theorizing it, however, literacy isn't contingent on ability. As I show in chapter 3, "Matters of the Closet," where I examine how the body can play a role in literacy, I find that ability is often connected to what crip theory has come to term *compulsory able-bodiedness*.[72] Ability carries baggage with it, which is debilitating for this project. Instead, I prefer the idea that literacy is an active, participatory force—moving, shifting, flowing, perhaps even alive in its own way. This is a point that's essential in understanding how literacies animate. The processual nature of literacy, often rendered as "reading and writing," has translated in my definition to *an exchange. Exchange* here is both noun and verb, a slippage I find beneficial. The action of an exchange highlights the literacy event. I'm not breaking away from conventional understanding of literacy events as having "interactional rules which regulate the type and amount of *talk* about what is written, and define ways in which *oral language* reinforces, denies, extends, or sets aside written material."[73] Rather, I would like to suggest that through queer agentiality, literacy events can also include energetic exchange between nontextual actors. It is in the exchange itself that animate literacies are found. You could say I'm indicating that literacy is shared among humans and nonhumans. At the same time, an exchange also implies a doing. Note that the purpose of the exchange is not transactional in the way you would exchange goods. The *exchange of forces* isn't product oriented but instead is caught up in a *flow*—a stark difference from understanding literacy as an economic resource or an ability alone.

Think of this flow as a current of factors and conditions that exist prior to the exchange, consisting as a *combination of sign systems, performances, and the sensate*. I use the metaphor of *flow* because it performs the fluid nature of literacy. Being literate is "coming to terms with the idea that nothing, even that which appears so convincingly solid ... is solid" and that worlds are a "kind of fluid" and "moving force."[74] With literacy, the flow isn't made up of reading, writing, and language alone. Animate literacies acknowledge the permeability and porousness of literacy actants and their potential to affect one another.

Moreover, literacy as caught up *in a flow* makes room for queer blockages, spillage, and leakage, which are important to animacies and, thus, also to my animation of literacy. I invoke water for its transmutative qualities, which in many ways are queer—water can shape-shift under necessary conditions, having in it at any given time the qualities of all states of matter, resisting any single form. Yet it is the basis of all life on earth. Framing literacy as flowing then subverts conventional ideas of literacy (as opposed to literacy being a tool or a resource or a technology) while also highlighting that it's a necessary component of life and not just of human life alone.

There are also particular ways of doing literacy that involve our bodies, even if oftentimes the body isn't present (e.g., my body is behind this screen typing these words, but my body will be missing when you read this), hence my addition of the *sensate* in the definition above. Literacy is felt, seen, heard, arguably even tasted. In short, literacy is sensational, as much as is it involved with language. I resist using *embodied sensation* in lieu of *sensate* because I want to avoid my human reader thinking of their own body first. On the contrary, *sensate* warrants pause to reconsider *what, not who*, can feel and sense. In this turn of phrase, the sensate can belong to the cycles of insects emerging, sensing, and singing from the earth or a plant that wilts from too little water. It could be that I'm wrong to include the sensate for other life forms. I realize that we can never truly know the other outside our own subjective experience. At the very least, though, turning away from sensation insofar as embodiment is concerned puts us in a space to think about how matterings and even sensations have a life of their own.

I do acknowledge, however, that where there is a body—when the sensate *is embodied*—the body always is in some place. Literacy is an exchange of forces *in and through particular places*. This is the topic I expand on in the next chapter, especially in reference to Appalachia. One way I animate literacies is to treat place as actively shaping the flow of literacy. If I am treating literacy almost akin to water in that it's fluid, place acts much like a container for the exchange of forces to occur; literacy fills up certain places in different ways. Notice, too, that bodies are not the only actors participating in my definition. In the conventional perspectives of literacy, as I've hoped to show, the exchange of literacy (i.e., "reading" and "writing") occurs between individuals. I've included, with the human, the nonhuman to decenter humanistic models of literacy and emphasize that by paying attention to other entities in literacy, literacy pushes its ontological perspectives even further.

Reading, Writing, and Queer Survival offers a model of literacy that responds to Brandt and Clinton's suggestion that "we need perspectives that show the various hybrids, alliances, and multiple agents and agencies that simultaneously occupy acts of reading and writing."[75] If literacy is *an exchange of forces, which flows* among many types of agents, then literacy, I argue, is involved with *effecting change* and *creating new ways of being with and meaning-making*. Being with and meaning-making are both concerned with living, being, even thriving among others in a myriad of matterings and affects—objects (sentient or not), bodies, animals, desire, and so on—but doing so meaningfully.

Herein, whenever I discuss *literacy*, I'm drawing from this more nuanced interpretation. And when I mention *animate literacies*, I am highlighting that, to shift our definition of literacy to a model that takes the nonhuman seriously, queerness is key. The entities that cannot language through humanistic means must not be taken for granted. Animate literacies disrupt the harmony around the binary of reading and writing, which takes too seriously human exceptionalism as its bread and butter.

The play on *animate* as a modifier of *literacies* in my project's title is intentional: as adjective and verb, *animate* echoes animacies theory's play with meaning and at the same time simultaneously asks my reader to reconsider who has agency in the model of animate literacies. If we treat *animate* as solely descriptive, then *literacies* is enlivened, suggestively more alive on its own than if it were the verb. In its second, verb-state meaning, you could say I make a request of my reader. I'm asking you *to animate* literacies with me. The slippage of meaning here is meant to lurk behind the premise of animate literacies that we do not write ourselves into the world alone; reading the world isn't privileged only to us bipedal ilk. The world also reads and writes us.

2

Queer Appalachia and Queer Stories

The first time I saw Gran'ma, she was wearing a threadbare dress. I'm guessing it was so shabby because of the many hand washings or lack of money to buy a new one. It was speckled with flowers, perhaps daisies or some relative of petunias. On her feet were house shoes while she scuttled along the exposed floorboards of her cabinlike home. I sat next to my mom in awe as my maternal great-grandmother—my mom's dad's mom—attempted to yell over the many other cousins, aunts, and uncles huddled about a cast-iron stove, which sat in the middle of the living room. "That's just how they talk, Caleb," Mom explained once we left. Mom and I never yelled at each other. Yelling was left to my dad. Even then, he scolded under his breath before he struck me for listening to Prince or wearing Granny's dress to protest church on Sundays. No. Gran'ma Saylor and that side of Mom's family were simply just loud.

It was the first and last time I saw her. Yet, still, I remember what I asked her before we left: "Why do you have so many locks on your door, Gran'ma?" Being about four years old and looking up at the weathered doorframe towering above me, I saw there were at least twelve locks of all sorts—not just padlocks and deadbolts, but she had the jimmy-proof sort, latches that locked, even the thin sliding locks you'd maneuver through the maze of metal nooks to snap shut. In the corner next to the door sat a shotgun. I didn't ask about it. It was obvious she meant to keep people out. I still to this day never discovered why she had so many locks.

Tucked away near the Kentucky Cumberland region, this was the town where my mom grew up: fewer than 850 people and rural. Like Gran'ma's door, that side of the family had always been locked away from me. I didn't have the lexical capacity to know why it was important for the family to keep outsiders out or why yelling was a way of talking. Or why my mom's moonshiner dad would resist electricity, refuse twenty-first-century medicine, and would eventually die because he refused a hospital visit. They were not me. But now, over two decades years later, I realize they were more connected to me than I realized because we both are Appalachian.

We were divided among ourselves; my mom and I were set apart from that side of the family. Mom moved away. She traveled around the country, following my dad while he was in the military, and at some point lived in Italy for three years. Technically, I'm a Yankee if you take into consideration that I was born a military brat in New York. I came back to Kentucky on my mom's hip when I was a few months old. I wasn't born in Appalachia, but, still, I am Appalachian. My point isn't to belabor family origins. Nor is it to say that Mom's side is Appalachian *only* because they were isolated, private people or yelled or made moonshine. My point is that I realize Appalachia is fraught with contradictions. Sometimes Appalachia doesn't make sense. There's a queerness in them there mountains.

This chapter begins there: queer Appalachia. I look to what can make Appalachia a region, identity, and culture—refusing any one stable marker besides the mountains themselves. In particular, and with regard to *Reading, Writing, and Queer Survival*, I am interested not only in what could make Appalachia queer but also how we can treat the mountains as queer agents. I suggest that we can expand the story of literacy studies, one that uses a framework of interconnectedness to see how the land and mountains and landscapes are alive, how places like Appalachia are agential as literacy sponsors.

Why Queer Appalachia?

The Appalachian Mountain range is one consistent factor in determining what is Appalachia. The mountains run from the bottom of Maine, curving like a backward C through Pennsylvania, southeast Ohio, the entire state of West Virginia, the western border of Virginia, parts of the Carolinas, the east halves of Kentucky and Tennessee, and ending at the tip of Alabama and Georgia. It's incredibly important to note that just because there are *the* Appalachian Mountains, it doesn't follow that there are such things as *the* Appalachian culture and identity. There are, instead, Appalachia*s*.

Appalachia is a polymorphism anchored by geography.[1] This becomes clear in most recent critical scholarship about the area: "Appalachia as a place has been so difficult to define that some have suggested that it is more akin to an idea than a geographic locale."[2] But it isn't simple enough to be rendered completely an idea because "Appalachia is both a real place to those who live there and a sometimes mythic land to outsiders," and for those who do live in Appalachia, "how they identify themselves varies from person to person."[3] One attempt to outline clearer edges describes four stereotypical images of Appalachia as being *"pristine Appalachia,* the unspoiled mountains and hills along the Appalachian trail . . . *backwater Appalachia,* home of the 'strange land and peculiar people' in thousands of stories, novels, radio and TV programs and films . . . *Anglo-Saxon Appalachia,* once defined by *Merriam-Webster's Collegiate Dictionary* as a mountain region of 'white natives' . . . *pitiful Appalachia,* the poster region of welfare and privation."[4]

The last image of poverty being synonymous with Appalachia rings more authentic than any other definition but not because it's wholly truthful. Appalachia was defined as a region, at least in terms of official policy, because of the federal government's "aide" of money and resources. The incorrect characterization of Appalachia as a primarily white region is demonstrably false. The large Scots-Irish antebellum migration to the mountains is oftentimes the given explanation as to why Appalachia is predominately white, but this narrative has been critiqued a number of times by researchers. There were Scots-Irish immigrants, but there were also German, French, Welsh, Dutch, and Scot immigrants, among other nationalities and ethnicities.[5]

More important, however, in regard to race, the homogenized myth surrounding whiteness ignores the Indigenous peoples who occupied the mountains for 10,000 years before pioneer settlement.[6] And while slavery was present in Appalachia during the late nineteenth century, it was complicated in the Appalachian region, with both "slave and free" Blacks reaching a population of roughly 175,000 and growing post–Civil War.[7] Ultimately, the "Scots-Irish heritage [of Appalachia] is real . . . but the exaggerated dominance of its influence in the region is often put into the service of a variety of outcomes," including racism and settler colonialism.[8]

In exploring why Appalachia has been linked to stereotypical images of poverty, I have yet to find any Appalachian scholarship that doesn't reference, minimally in passing or through lengthy remonstration, the Appalachian Regional Commission—the ARC, established in 1965 during the Johnson administration's War on Poverty. It was the ARC that defined Appalachia as a distinct area of the United States in terms of legislation. I'd summarize the motivation for the ARC's formation as being ultimately driven by the exploitation of economic and political resources and labor. It concealed its true purpose behind the visage of a philanthropic mission to save an entire region from poverty.[9] By ARC's design, "the region came to be defined by poverty, and subsequently poverty came to be defined by the region."[10]

The relationship between poverty and Appalachia lingers still. You'll find it in the stories that follow. If I haven't made it clear, I grew up poor from Appalachia. Appalachia isn't *only* poor; the reason the region is cast this way is because it was, in part, defined by our national narrative as such. I'm in agreement with other scholars on this point: "Appalachian scholars and activists often prefer to stress our interconnectedness to other regions and peoples rather than set ourselves apart as exceptions."[11] I'm not sure if I would be shunned among Appalachian scholars for saying it, but I find all the definitions above resonate with my experience in some way. Appalachia *is* romanticized because it *is* beautiful; *is* poor in places; *is* in need of restoration, especially with regard to the land; *is* racist like the rest of the United States, littered with Confederate memorabilia and racist hate groups. But it isn't *just* one or all or always those things. Perhaps that's the point, though. There isn't a single way to define what it means *to be* Appalachian.

Appalachia has been cast as one of America's *others* for quite some time. You could say that its othered status was in part shaped by the ARC's influence, but mostly the othered status has been formed by outsiders looking and coming in. After the Civil War, capitalism sunk its teeth into the region, marking Appalachia as a place to be saved with the promises of modernity, which should be understood as profit. Whether it was academics who come to study Appalachians, corporations that exploit land for coal and resources, or the government that subsidizes health care, welfare, and education, Appalachia in the cultural imagination is simultaneously set apart from America and deeply part of it. As one scholar puts it, "We *know* Appalachia exists because we need it to exist in order to define what we are not."[12] A parallel can be drawn with this point here to similar arguments about queerness in regard to straightness.

Whether queer theorists draw from Rich's compulsory heterosexuality or by way of Foucault's repressive hypothesis, there's a notion in queer theory that through queerness, straightness is propagated and reified as the norm. In other words, straightness needs queerness to set it apart, just like America needs Appalachia to set its dominant culture apart.[13] Although don't mistake me. I'm not implying Appalachia's queerness is the same type as sexual or gender nonnormativity (although it certainly can be). This doesn't mean that to be Appalachian is to be queer read as nonstraight, either; homo-/trans-/queerphobia and queer hate crimes are just as prevalent in Appalachia as they are elsewhere in the United States. It is in otherness, strangeness, indeterminacy, and resistance that Appalachia and queerness overlap.[14] And this leads me to my point: Appalachia is queer. Appalachia is a queer place. Those who identify as Appalachian know this, I've found. Appalachia identities exist, but it's incredibly difficult to spell out what it means to be Appalachian. Appalachia is queer because it's just as slippery an identificatory category. The trickiness and contradiction that surround Appalachia as a region and identity aren't the only premises to warrant its queerness, though.

Working under the assumption that Appalachia is a queer place and to be Appalachian is to be queer in its own way, I still haven't addressed *why* I chose Appalachia as the site of my research. I am an Appalachian queer who bought into the fable that to be Appalachian and to be successful is to leave Appalachia. "To leave," as Catte critiques it, "is to demonstrate our ambition, to be something other than dependent and stubborn. To leave is to be productive rather than complacent, and to refuse is to be complicit."[15] It cannot be overstated how Appalachians have a bad reputation for being dependent and lazy, expectant of aide, lacking motivation—all factors grossly misrepresenting and overlooking how this narrative began. Appalachia was long a piecemeal part of my identity, encroaching but never fully actualized till graduate school. I didn't want to be associated with where I grew up. I actively worked to muffle my dialect. I sought higher education as a ticket "to get the hell outta here," as my mom would say. I came out young, at fourteen, as a huge *FUCK YOU* to everyone around me. Reading and writing and being in the top of my class all through elementary, middle, and high school took priority so I could "make something of myself."[16]

I worked so hard to not be the stereotypes of where I lived during my first eighteen years, even if I didn't know I was Appalachian at the time. I realize now that I was struggling with the stereotypes of Appalachia. I didn't know I was Appalachian until I wasn't. This only occurred to me when I was faced with the question all academics must ask at some point: Why does your research matter? Before I could answer, I realized Appalachia was a hole in my life. It was a place on a map that I tried to cover up with a college degree, choke out with standardized English, and erase by moving to the city. "You're from Kentucky? But you don't sound like it," an undergrad English professor once said to me. Still, I can hear her and see where I stood when I was caught for being from rural Kentucky years ago. Now I'm returning to Appalachia not to fix some problem there but to understand why, on some level and in some instances, it's considered a problem for Appalachians to be Appalachian.

Asking Other Questions, or Being With

Most definitions, studies, and pedagogies of literacy, especially in American contexts, have propagated literacy with human apogee, and we are so inculcated by this spawning of human exceptionalism that we need wider ways of being to bring the nonhuman into our worldview. What if "rather than limit our analyses to one creature at a time (including humans), or even one relationship, if we want to know what makes a place livable we should be studying polyphic assemblages, gatherings as a way of being."[17] Which is to say, not only do we study literacy through analytics like literacy sponsorship or the literacy narrative; we must also examine such devices as part of a larger story. This section explores another way of thinking of the world, as interconnected, vital, and emergent, to eventually reach another means of approaching literacy and literacy practices as animated, particularly in a region so alive as Appalachia.

How do we come to face nonhuman actors as equals and accept we don't have to have all the answers, which even physics has shown isn't possible? It requires a radical shift from divisive thinking. No longer is it us humans, in here, and nature, with its nonhumans, out there. We must come to terms with the notion that no matter how much we divide up the world into pieces, smaller and smaller, imagining we will arrive at the truth like an infinite Russian nesting doll hiding the truth in its innermost chamber, we will never find it. Instead, animate literacies propose the thinking of *being with*, as I call it, or, as new materialist Karen Barad names it, intra-action: "The object and the measuring agencies emerge from, rather than precede, the intra-action that produces them."[18] Barad is discussing the relationship between tools and their users in quantum physics when she coins this term *intra-action*. Besides quantum mechanics having its own magical reasoning, my point is simply that it requires an alternative worldview to entertain and accept that we may never know that outside ourselves, but we mustn't see ourselves as wholly separate either.[19] Meaning emerges from the actions between us and the world. This alternate view—animate literacies' *being with*—could be described as "the form of an onto-story," where things have "thing-power: the curious ability of inanimate things to animate, to act, to produce effect dramatic and subtle": "Picture an ontological field without any unequivocal demarcations between human, animal, vegetable, or mineral. All forces and flows (materialities) are or can become lively, affective, and signaling. . . . This field lacks primordial divisions, but it is not a uniform or flat topography. It is just that its differentiations are too protean and diverse to coincide exclusively with the philosophical categories of life, matter, mental, environmental. . . . In this onto-tale, everything is, in a sense, alive."[20]

We need other ways of telling stories, "protean and diverse," a critical function of onto-stories, which reveal to us that the world has already and always been a participant. In other words, we don't have to imbue the nonhuman actors with agency in this approach to literacy because they've been there the entire time; it only requires us to pay attention to supplement the already broad field of literacy studies. The human isn't above the world but a part of it; intra-action, then, is a matter of relationships constantly emerging. Furthermore, the literacies we have in academia aren't always accessible to everyone. We need new ways of thinking about being with our world that don't necessitate a college education. To be with the world around us, you could say, is a literacy of immanence—recognizing the, at times, porous but always malleable boundaries between self and other in the immediate world. The story of literacy changes with being with.

When I say literacy forms between actors, it requires a rewired worldview that being with one another and others is "webbed, tentacular, knotted," and not linear.[21] Literacy is the flow of energies pulling us together in meaningful ways but also emerges simultaneously from those relationships. Jeannette Armstrong, an Indigenous Okanagan scholar, writes on this point: "The Okanagan word for 'our place on the land' and 'our language' is the same. This means that the land has taught us our language. The way we survived is to speak the languages that the land offered us as its teachings.... We also refer to the land and our bodies with the same root syllable. This means that the flesh which is our body is pieces of the land come to us through the things which the land is."[22]

Armstrong demonstrates how literacy forms through relationality. Moreover, through the energetic flow of literacy, relationships among body, place, land, and language are formed for the Okanagan peoples. Literacies animated are emergent through multiple relations, not merely those relationships of human-to-human or human-to-human-written text. The nebulous assemblage of animate literacy practices is ongoing and not merely belonging to humans.

If literacy is emergent, we cannot actively go out in search of it in the way literacy scholars have commonly asked the question, *Who taught you to read and write?* Instead, we must ask for stories based around objects and affects and wait for literacy to announce itself. I propose we look to queer stories as potent places to discover how the world has been a part of literacy all along, animating it. It isn't merely that we use language to represent the world; representation and meaning work both ways in the metaphor. As a result, the metaphors used in stories can offer a way into the recesses of how new modes of relationality occur, and it takes a bit of magical thinking to discover these metaphors. I propose, then, that we take up metaphor and a new analytic of finding those metaphors in stories—what I come to define as *metaphoric tracking*—to think of literacy otherwise.

How are animate literacies enacted as a methodology? Where can animate literacies be found? Maybe, even, who should care? And how do I study it? I'd like to clarify that *methodology* and *methods*, as I use the terms, are distinct from one another while simultaneously always linked. When I say *methodology*, I think of two questions: Why do we study the way we do? And how do we plan to study in such a way? When I say *methods*, I'm referring to the actual everyday practice of the research, where a "method is a technique for (or way of proceeding in) gathering evidence," while "methodology is a theory and analysis of how research does or should proceed."[23] Extending my expanded definition of literacy in chapter 1, I argue that the *being with* or relationality of animate literacies can best be analyzed through metaphors or, as I call it, *metaphoric tracking*.

Metaphoric tracking is a method of listening and searching for metaphors in queer storytelling. It shifts the methodological questions of literacy studies from only *Who taught us to read and write?* and *What or how do we read and write?* to a question of *How do we use literacy to read and write* the world *around us?* And, more radically, *What ways has the world written us?* Metaphoric tracking looks at affects and matterings in metaphors to offer an alternative model of analyzing literacy, which explores the agency of matter and affect.

Queer Storytelling as Methodology

We should always begin with story. Storytelling isn't just the medium through which Appalachians are known to make meaning and art, but it also gets us as close as we can, I believe, to that which cannot be captured in language. Even by telling the story, you never capture the original setting, context, audience, environment in toto. In its retelling, details of the events change, locations both in the story perhaps and where you're telling it again, the reason for telling the story changes. The story is slippery, immediate, and fleeting. The refutation of this, I realize, is that we read stories, too, making them appear more fixed insofar as we can sometimes touch them—still, even when we read a story, we change as individuals from reading to reading. The stories we read take on different meanings during different parts of our lives, along with why we reread and with whom we share the stories, in print or otherwise. Storytelling is messy.

In this way, storytelling and queerness are correlative. "If the term 'queer' is to be a collective contestation, the point of departure for a set of historical reflections and futural imaginings," Butler writes in her earlier work, "it will have to remain that which is, in the present, never fully owned, but always and only redeployed, twisted, and queered from a prior usage and in the direction of urgent and expanding political purposes, and perhaps also yielded in favor of terms that do that political work more effectively."[24]

Queer is "never fully owned," always denying meaning but constantly a referent that functions in no single part of speech and writing. I am a queer, *a noun*. I queer literacy studies in this project, *a verb*. This chapter is concerned with my queer methodology, *an adjective*.

Queer, as Butler suggests above, is always deployed in the present responding to a politicized past and possibilities of meaning in the future. Butler mentions that queer's valences are always political. When I think of politics, I think of power: Who has it? Why? And how can we resist it when necessary? The stories in *Reading, Writing, and Queer Survival* become political in that they help frame the literacy of queers, of Appalachia, and of Appalachian queers. I am asking how queer Appalachian storytelling resists stereotypical narratives of Appalachia while at the same time giving queers the agency and power to tell their own stories.

Labeling my primary method and methodology of "data" collection *queer storytelling* is a politically charged decision, too, because (1) it resists typical patriarchal, white, heteronormative academic approaches that don't always embrace storytelling as serious business, and (2) it also embraces queerness at every level—researcher, participant, theory, methodology, and method, even genre and medium. My methodology agrees with Halberstam that "a queer methodology is, in a way, a scavenger methodology that uses different methods to collect and produce information" and "attempts to combine methods that are often cast as being at odds with each other," resisting "academic compulsion toward disciplinary coherence."[25] The words *queer* and *mess* aren't "limited to bodies, objects, and desires" but also point out "processes, behaviors, and situations."[26]

As I see it, in order to truly embrace queer research, we have to be willing to improvise when situations for detour present themselves while we are collecting queer stories. We must be willing to get messy. Here are a few ways my research became messy, where I let the stories of my participants animate my research: the interview questions at times turned irrelevant during the interview when many of my participants told stories that took my research in different directions—we'd chat about families and locations; we'd both agree on painful experiences or reminisce about special places in Appalachia. Honesty in the face of pain is another instance where the research took queer turns, loosening the interview setting into something akin to meeting a stranger in a bar.

Two main concepts come to mind with regard to my queer methodology: *transparency* and *reciprocity*. Transparency on some level breaks through the public/private divide. Queerness and mess would press the boundaries of transparency, risking visibility between researcher/participants, reader/writer, public/private as well as understanding that visibility is not always stable. In this way, transparency becomes a praxis, with *praxis* being understood as "research that privileges neither the theoretical foundation nor the observed practice."[27] By framing transparency as a praxis, I take strides to ensure that my participants have maximum involvement with their stories that I discuss and showcase. Before any publications, final drafts, or any material is used of my participants' stories, I contacted my participants, allowing them to make comments, question my representation of their narrative, and even withdraw after the fact.

Scholars in rhetoric, composition, and literacy research have taken reciprocity as a critical component of person- and community-based research.[28] I certainly don't lose sight of its importance here. Reciprocity concerns itself with relationships: "A theory of reciprocity, then, frames this activist agenda with a self-critical, conscious navigation of this intervention."[29] Reciprocity is linked in large part to feminist epistemologies: "This nonhierarchical, reciprocal relationship, in which both researcher and researched learn from one another and have a voice in the study, is informed by a feminist desire for eliminating power inequalities between researchers and participants and a concern for the difficulties of speaking for 'the other.'"[30] Queer theory, by extension, does the same with calling into question normative sexualities and bodies. Working under the assumption that feminist methods derive from gender analytics, I must ask: What would reciprocity look like if queer methods come from taking nonnormative sex and sexuality as a point of theoretical analysis? Put another way, what does queer reciprocity look like if we are taking the bawdy and the salacious as sites of analysis?

I'm not entirely sure I can answer those questions. Perhaps I can't fully sketch out the contours of queer reciprocity because there isn't any method that is inherently queer; instead, "all methods can be put to queer political ends that disrupt normative alignments."[31] This highlights animacies theory's use of queer being volatile and unstable as a category. Violating any "proper" use, queer is elusive, refusing, resisting, and contradicts any stable method. But queers have stories. Ultimately, my point is this: there needs to be some anchor or center of gravity to study literacy in such a queer new way, and queer stories can be such a site. Simply put, the queer methodology I am suggesting—collecting queer stories based on transparency and reciprocity—deals with uncomfortable topics. This may, for some readers, cause pause or bring up ethically complex areas around sex and sexuality. My methodology relies on writing, interacting, and researching as transparently as possible despite how uncomfortable it may be for all persons involved.

Perhaps what I'm grappling with concerning queer transparency and queer reciprocity is also desiring new ways to think of and new methodologies of studying literacy: "But I'm also wanting to know what might happen if we turn attention to literacy as ways of being not just sponsored (and hence extorted or suppressed), but also desired. What methodologies might we develop to account for the ways in which some of us have had to seek out new ways of being literate in the world? . . . How might the promises of literacy be experienced differently if we understand literacy as a thing *desired*?"[32]

To desire something or someone in ways that aren't acceptable or deemed normative is to desire queerly but may not necessarily be queer desire. Alexander's understanding that literacy can be a thing worth desiring mustn't be lost in a queer study of literacy. If we think of desiring literacy, it may be helpful insofar as how we ask our questions in our methodologies. This exposes literacy as a thing unto itself, "a thing desired." What would it mean to desire Appalachia in other ways too? What does it mean for us researchers when our own stories are so knotted into the place of our research that we can't help but question who we are when we ask, "What is it that we study?" This can have some implications as far as how we approach our research. In fact, I'd like to offer that queer reciprocity doesn't end with the relationship between participant and researcher but instead extends further between researcher and reader.

A queer ethic of transparency and reciprocity would extend to you, my reader. As a writer developing a theory of animate literacies where literacy has a life of its own, I cannot ignore the agency of my words once they're read. As such, it should be desired that literacy animated would acknowledge openly and honestly the relationship among participants, researcher, reader, and writer on all levels. Granted, you can't directly write back or speak to me as far as reading this on a page. However, I can attempt to be as transparent by clearly articulating the motives behind my actions. This requires of me to be honest about my position to my research, any biases I may have, and the processes involved in doing this work; it requires reciprocity between me and my participants, even if that means simply listening to painful memories. Moreover, I believe if animate literacies are deploying queer storytelling as a methodology, it requires that the researcher take their own queer subjectivity into question—the researcher's queer storytelling is part and parcel to a queer methodology.

What this may look like regarding genre conventions could vary, but at its heart, I believe that the self is always called into question, as writer, researcher, participant, and reader. While mulling over the possibility of writing a queer self in their digital text *Techne*, Alexander and Rhodes "understand queer *composing* as a queer rhetorical practice aimed at disrupting how we understand ourselves to ourselves. As such, it is a composing that is not a composing, a call in many ways to acts of de- and un- and re-composition."[33] Let's widen their argument, here, to queer methodological research as well: queer methods should disrupt how we research our research. What would it mean to de-search, un-search, re-research? From the perspective of animacy theory, the suffixes here point out adverbial agency: *de-* from the Latin for *from, down, away*; *un-*, synonymous at times with *in-* and *non-*, meaning *not, to undo, reverse*, or *do the opposite*; *re-*, which points us *back, backward*, to do *again, anew*.

As a methodological framework for literacy research, then, queer storytelling would seek to look to the periphery of typical studied sites of literacy—what surrounds the texts and pedagogy, as it were. It would undo, reverse, and be in contrast with previous methodological approaches, always looking backward in order to think *again* about the basis for approaches to studying literacy. When Alexander writes of how he learned to be queerly literate "*outside* a formal curriculum," he states, "These elements—work on digital platforms, the experience of collaboration, and acculturation across a lifespace—are other dimensions of literacy that need more nuanced attention, particularly as they are often pursued simultaneously by many people in many different situations and contexts. We need methodologies that will better track the development of these kinds of literacies. We need a phenomenological approach that will account better for the complexities of literacies that are not just sponsored, but that emerge out of deep needs for affinity and affiliation."[34]

A critical requirement of deploying queer storytelling is learning to listen and be receptive and to actively engage in the process of listening both during the person-to-person interaction and *in the writing of the storytelling*. If we need more nuanced means of coming to literacy, then we need to recognize that we must undo our perceptions of what constitutes literacy from the get-go. Animate literacies take up queer stories because to be receptive, to listen, to attempt to locate the role of the nonhuman in our literacy practices is to acknowledge that literacy isn't the mere ability to read and write, and literacy isn't exclusively human—and in this way, Appalachia is alive, animated.

Stories are queer because they resist a Westernized and, by proxy, deeply messianic way of knowing and being. They animate theory by blatantly refusing to adhere to qualified knowledge-making of declarative empiricism. Lee Maracle, an Indigenous Canadian writer, scholar, and poet, points out plainly, "Academicians waste a great deal of effort deleting character, plot, and story from theoretical argument," elucidating that storytelling is "in every line of theory."[35] By paying attention to story, animate literacies' focus on and incorporation of other constituents of literacy become a performance of sorts like the critical storytelling of the recently emergent field of cultural rhetorics. Storytelling, both in format and in content, highlights the reciprocity and transparency that I've unpacked so far because "people make meaning through relationships that are always constellated.... The practice of relationality changes throughout that process, and is made visible in multiple ways."[36] "The practice of relationality" holds a considerable amount of bearing on my methodology à la animate literacies' relation to the nonhuman. Next, I hope to bring into clearer focus how looking at queer metaphors can act as an opportunity to study literacy in a new light.

Metaphor as Relation, Metaphor as Method

The question lingers from the previous first half of this book: how do we approach the nonhuman on their own terms? Through engaging new materialism, I've suggested queer literacy can help us in decentering our humanistic tendencies. We cannot, I realize, succeed at completely removing the human out of literacy, although we can learn how to *be with* the nonhuman in more creative, *meaning-making* ways. Looking at stories and the metaphors used in storytelling, I propose a new materialist analytic tool to analyze literacy: *metaphoric tracking*.

Metaphoric tracking borrows from and adapts Laurie Gries's new materialist rhetorical method of iconographic tracking in visual rhetorics and circulation theories and applies similar tenets to queer animate literacies.[37] The metaphoric tracking method draws from actual stories, events, and individual experience, using the methodologies of queer storytelling as a point of departure and site of data analysis. Central to metaphoric tracking is the metaphor: "The essence of metaphor is understanding and experiencing one kind of thing in terms of another."[38] Moving away from the ability-resource model of literacy requires us to acknowledge that literacy exists in interactions; literacy is found in the ways of *being with* others, of experiencing one kind of experience in terms of another.

When it concerns metaphors of literacy, it's been noted how literacy is often discussed and researched with three metaphors in mind: literacy as adaptation, literacy as power, and literacy as a state of grace.[39] The first, dealing with adaptation, centers on functional literacy, or is "conceived broadly as the level of proficiency necessary for effective performance in a range of settings and customary activities." Functional literacy parallels what I've been calling the ability-resources model of literacy. There's an element of "common sense" to this metaphor—you need to be literate to function in mundane situations.[40] It suggests reading labels on medicine bottles or street signs while driving. Brushing off the mundaneness of literacy as adaptation risks homogenizing literacy acquisition and ignoring local, community-based literacy practices.

The second metaphor of literacy as power seems obvious and has been threaded throughout *Reading, Writing, and Queer Survival*: "literacy has been a potent tool in maintaining the hegemony of elites and dominant classes in certain societies."[41] Noting that while "masses of people have been mobilized for fundamental changes in social conditions . . . rapid extensions of literacy have been accomplished," the metaphor of literacy as power isn't primarily about personal empowerment even while it's often packaged as such.[42] This metaphor, I believe, has shifted in part to the individual. Black queer literacy scholar Eric Pritchard has made it apparent in their work that individuals have used literacy for self-empowerment, especially when literacy is bound up with race, gender, and sexuality. This isn't to say that literacy as power has elided state power and hierarchies of oppression, but access to new literacies often enables new modes of self-agency. Whenever literacy as power, notice, has been used as a metaphor, its focus is on the power of humans alone. It's also a matter of human ownership. I'd like to think that animate literacies as a theory can broaden our understanding of how power, like agency, could be shared between actants. Literacy is powerful for Appalachians—or can be. A few examples come to mind: the way my nanny would collect genealogies in the family Bible or the way that my mom taught me to budget money at a young age "because we have to survive, Caleb." The participants will demonstrate this too. I'd reckon there are other ways Appalachians are literate, through our folxways, which I teach students and discuss in the final chapter.

Last, the metaphor of literacy as a state of grace reinforces my examination of literacy studies' tendency to treat literacy as transcending the inanimate world: "the tendency in many societies to endow the literate person with special virtues" has both religious and broader, secular implications.[43] Despite the literacy myth being disproved (see Graff), literacy's state of grace metaphor requires us to question, even today, if literacy still "creates a great divide in intellectual abilities between those who have and those who have not mastered written language."[44] This metaphoric analysis highlights the importance of paying attention to how we talk about literacy and the language used in studying it. We must be careful how we discuss literacy, then, in the context of Appalachians too—literacy doesn't have to set us free because we are already literate in ways other Americans aren't. Adding to this position would mean accepting "that metaphor is pervasive in everyday life, not just in language but in thought and action. Our ordinary conceptual system, in terms of which we both think and act, is fundamentally metaphorical in nature."[45] What if instead of looking at the metaphors we use to theorize literacy, we looked at the metaphors people use in the stories they tell about their own literacies—especially those literacies that extend beyond traditional reading and writing?

Metaphoric tracking looks for metaphors in queer storytelling as indicators of relationality on all levels. Metaphors of reading and writing alone aren't enough. Metaphoric tracking seeks out two specific types of metaphors, what I'm terming *literacy affects* and *literacy matters* to support my theoretical approach to literacy. Literacy affects are metaphors in queer stories pointing to ways of being affected and affecting others and, most distinctly, how affects can linger and perhaps have a tempo-spatial lifespan. Literacy affects deal with subjectivity. Identity is often bound up with the emotive states made apparent by storytellers. Literacy affects would also explain how affects can stick to places.[46] Think back to my dream at the beginning. The nightmares of "a deep abyss" affected my waking world; however, they failed to accurately represent it (there wasn't a deep abyss outside, and I wasn't in my grandparents' house). This failure to make sense of these dreams is arguably queer: I made new meaning by way of these dreams or, more accurately, by being haunted by them until I discovered my Appalachian grandfather had passed. Through the literacy affect of a nightmare, I also created a new way to be with my grandmother because I came out to her that very same day.

Literacy matters, on the one hand, emerge out of relation to objects, matter, and place. Literacy matters look for relations *in and through places.* Literacy matters also pay attention to how *performance and the sensate* are critical in animating literacy. I'm tempted to say literacy matters are metaphors of the tangible here, too, but fear it risks being reductive, for some objects aren't tangible. For instance, air and sunlight and climate change are still objects, just not tactile in the sense we can press against them or pick them up. Take the literacy matter from my story where the "mountain got up and left"—clearly a metaphor because mountains indeed don't walk, yet through the metaphor, I acknowledge the mountain's agency in my story as well as how literacy failed in terms of my relationship with my grandfather; I never had the opportunity to tell him how I prayed for the mountain to move.

Metaphor tracking is a method of literacy research where actively seeking out metaphors in storytelling reveals relationships in lived lives, exposing how being with others (both human and nonhuman) shapes literacy and creates meaning. The metaphor is a temporal-spatial container, meaning that metaphors are always situated in the space of different things, and they change over time. From this temporal-spatial understanding come three particular types of metaphors, which animate literacies will rely on in their method of analysis: structural, orientational, and ontological.

Structural metaphors are "cases where one concept is metaphorically structured in terms of another."[47] Structural metaphors are situated in systems and are thus reliant on the structures that give them meaning. For instance, in capitalistic thinking, it is commonplace to say that *time is money*. We can only understand this in a system such as capitalism where you are paid for your time. Outside of the systems they reference, structural metaphors dissolve into nonsense, whereas orientational metaphors are spatial insofar as they proceed from our bodily experience in direct relationship to place and time. Orientational metaphors "arise from the fact that we have bodies of the sort we have and that they function as they do in our physical environment."[48]

Last, ontological metaphors uncover modes of being and ways that literacy discloses what can exist and what cannot because "once we can identify our experiences as entities or substance, we can refer to them, categorize them, group them, and quantify them—and, by this means, reason about them."[49] The literacy sponsor, by this way of thinking, even acts as a metaphor. An individual who "is" a literacy sponsor only becomes a literacy sponsor retroactively through literacy research's container metaphor of the literacy sponsor itself. The person *isn't* a literacy sponsor ontologically speaking but becomes such through metaphor. Thinking through ontological metaphors is difficult because they're so innocuous and are the basis for our everyday lives—we must think of our existence in terms of metaphors to process information. Methodologically speaking, metaphoric tracking must be wary of overlooking ontological metaphors that we may take for granted because of how ingrained they are in our collective stories. As far as *Reading, Writing, and Queer Survival* is concerned, I actively look for blocked meaning in metaphors, metaphors that shouldn't exist, or, in other words, from my participants' stories, I look for these structural, orientational, and ontological metaphors that are queer in all the ways I have engaged thus far. I see these three types of metaphors working next to and correlating with certain aspects of the new framework of literacy I proposed in chapter 1.

The method of metaphoric tracking looks for these three metaphors in particular ways within storytelling. For structural metaphors, metaphoric tracking looks to phrases, statements, and questions where meaning is contingent on systems, cultural understanding, or context. Much like how *time is money* is a metaphor that speaks to a larger system of capitalism, metaphors that rely on meaning derived from broader cultural references make clear how animate literacies emanate from a combination of sign systems, performances, and the sensate. In the queer stories I collected, I looked for contingent meaning in the language my participants used to tell their stories.

Metaphors that deploy "I" statements and/or rely on *to be*, no matter what tense, to declare two unlike things similar through difference expose ontological metaphors. Metaphoric tracking would actively seek out moments in stories where states of being are coupled through the relationship between various literacy actors. These metaphors can be personal, or they can point to the relationship between other things. Orientational metaphors are perhaps the easiest to catch, with prepositions being their primary identifying marker. Grounded in experience, orientational metaphors point out how literacy arrives in relationships of actors. Take this example: I breathe *in* the flower. "In" as a preposition brings together myself and the flower. Via prepositions, we understand, too, the relationship to place and how we navigate it. Looking at orientational metaphors, we can see how queerness denies typical animacy hierarchies and reorients how literacy flows in and through particular places. Adverbial clauses also have a role to play in orientational metaphors. Answering questions such as *Where? When? How? To what extent?*, adverbs distinguish types of spatial relationships. Adverbs do not require objects but still carry with them the weight of orientational metaphors.

Through metaphoric tracking, I'm particularly interested in moments when language fails to account for queer experiences, and new metaphors arise as a result. As I said at the beginning of this chapter, a queer methodological approach allows for interruptions and dialogues between researcher and storyteller. When I don't understand my participants, I interject to ask a question for clarity. I take note because these moments are where meaning has failed somehow. Both in my annotations during these moments and in the story themselves, I look at these instances for metaphors. Notwithstanding the researcher's note-taking, a transcription of stories is necessary to look for metaphors.

Searching for metaphors in the transcriptions isn't easy and often takes multiple readings or listening to recordings many times, as detailed in the prologue. For this reason, I've narrowed the focus, tracking metaphors related to four aspects of queer literacies: trauma, bodies, places, and spirituality. Importantly, metaphoric tracking isn't limited to these four categories, and by the end of *Reading, Writing, and Queer Survival*, it'll become apparent that the possibilities of metaphoric tracking may very well go beyond what I am theorizing here.

Becoming a Night-Crowler

Animate literacies ask us to be suspect of literacy emerging solely and wholly through human sociality. It also requires us to not rule out that there are other ways literacies can be understood and thus studied. To put it plainly, literacy arises in part from our interactions with the matterings and affects around us. Animate literacies' methodology asks us to look at the literacies we use to tell our stories. To look back. Look away. Look again. And to do so as transparently as possible with literacy, with how we research it, with whom we research it, where we research it, and, most importantly, with ourselves. We don't have to take the story away from theory—stories are enough in themselves. We don't always have to rip flesh from stories, gnawing for bits of data bone deep, or mine for facts to the point that narrative arcs are demolished, flattened for their profit. Yet if we must and when we must look for data points, let's do so with an attempt to disrupt the verisimilitude of meaning-making devoid of story by seeking new metaphors and new ways of being with our literacies.

The interwoven testimonies of the queers I interview are full of metaphors, and that allows us to reconsider how we are to be with stories, and perhaps I'm attempting to do the same with you, my reader. In my research travels through Appalachia to collect queer stories, I drove through and spent a good spell in West Virginia. I wound through the serpentine backroads, drove alongside rivers, and even swam in the Appalachian watering holes between interviews during my downtime. I wanted to experience the land as I wrote and listened to the queer stories you'll read in the following pages.

Stopping at a convenience store, I caught the picture above on the door. Until I attempted to sound out *night-crowless*, I wasn't sure what the word meant. *Night-crowless* is a phonetic transcription of *nightcrawlers*, a type of earthworm often used in catching bottom feeders like catfish. I know because my father, whenever he forced me to fish on his farm, used to make fun of me for not wanting to pick up the bait worms, let alone pierce their muculent, writhing bodies with a fishing hook. Belonging to the phylum Annelida, Latin for *little ring*, earthworms are blind hermaphrodites who eat our organic garbage and surface from the ground when it rains. Their shit fuels our agriculture, especially in smaller, local farming and gardening. After I encountered that sign on that backroad, I knew that I had to relook and reconsider what I was doing in that very moment as a queer literacy researcher. What queerer figure to invoke than the earthworm in the way I navigate animate literacies in Appalachia?

Credit: Caleb Pendygraft

The sign resonates with what I'm in search of with my methodology. If I were a literacy scholar in a typical sense, I'd take night-crowless as an indication of failed semantics insofar as its meaning fails to be properly signed. But as a queer literacy scholar who's *also* Appalachian, I exalt night-crowless as precisely what I'm searching for in this queer project. So I am becoming not like the nightcrawler but the night-crowler. Queer and contradictory and inappropriate. Decomposing, blindly feeling around in the dark, I inch my way through these pages, taking what could be cast aside as wasteful, utter garbage, off-putting, or "not the stuff of literacy," and composting soil for new literacies to egress and grow, die, to transform again. Worms turn up when it rains so much the water sits atop the ground, so saturated it can't take any more in. Animate literacies don't place confidence in only humans being privy to literacy; literacy lives in the alluvium of queer relations and forms from the intra-animation of actors surviving among one another, a tangled mass of kinships so bound up and knotted it's difficult to discern its beginning or end. But what do I know? I'm only a night-crowler: misspelled and wrong in all the ways that shouldn't make sense but still insist on being, queerly slithering through these mountains.

3

Matters of the Closet

She laid out the cards one by one. I was sitting across a woman with a table between us, crammed into a small, repurposed utility closet. The dim lighting, noise of a water fountain, and ambient sounds of new-age woodwinds accompanied pungent incense—none of this seemed unusual to me at fifteen years old. The holy rolling of Pentecostals and the involvement with the occult were two mountain springs running off the same hill in my childhood. On the one side, I was used to hearing of demons and devils or listening to prophecies given during church service in some rural Kentucky garage. On the other, I would tag along with my mom to consult psychics all across Kentucky's hills and hollers, where she sought out sage wisdom through the shuffling of a pack of playing cards or tarot deck.

Once we drove for hours to see a granny witch far out in the mountains. With the gravel road crunching beneath my mom's car, I sat in the back seat. I can picture it still. The woman swayed back and forth in her rocking chair on the front porch. Chickens scurried about the yard, around a house that looked as though it was finished midconstruction. Someone threw slop out the front door while the woman stared down at my mom with one eye. The other was ghastly blue-white. She told us to go. She wasn't reading anyone today. Startled, we left. But there were other visits to various Kentucky augurs who surely could play the role.

The trips to the psychic in the trailer park stand out the most. Her single-wide was always filthy. My younger self had grown accustomed to sitting on the edge of the couch as to not contaminate myself in the grime and gunk or risk having a roach crawl across me. While she told my mom of cheating lovers and financial ruin to come, I would occasionally play with her grandkids. I'd use the opportunity to survey the entire house, fascinated with finding the new-age paraphernalia hidden among the morass of trash and clutter. Books filled with spells and sigils surreptitiously beckoned me to peruse their pages when I snuck off to a back room. Otherwise, I'd sit quietly and admire the stones she had placed in any available space. Yet what I'll never forget was once spotting the phallus-shaped candle that sat on a shelf in her bedroom closet, among piles of clothes and neglected grocery bags of who knows what. The wick stuck out the tip, and the entire candle, perhaps eight inches tall, was scarlet. What arcane or nefarious power did such an artifact possess? I was at once simultaneously fascinated and found it alluring, provoked by a desire that I couldn't name in my youth.

So when I say that I was accustomed to the atmospheric climate of new-age prognostication, I'm genuine. And the woman turning over cards at the table when I was fifteen was not the first to do so. This tarot reading, however, shaped the rest of my life. She read my cards and told me that I would be a teacher someday. I struggle to remember what cards she turned over that led her to that conclusion. Did she turn over the Magician? Standing tall, pointing upward with his wand, his other hand gesturing to the ground beneath him. Crowned with a lemniscate, the Magician teaches how energy can never be destroyed, only transformed. On his altar before him, all four symbols of the tarot and their corresponding elements: the wand, representing fire and spirit; the chalice, which holds the element of water; a sword, with its ability to slice through air; and the pentacle, the physical representation of money and earthly gains. Or was it the Chariot? The soldier behind the reins of the Chariot is drawn by two oppositely colored sphinxes, ancient guardians of balanced wisdom. The Chariot promises that, through tempered action and the ethical control of forces in one's life, victory awaits at the end of a long, hard journey. Would teaching bring me from rags to riches, as the Chariot promises? While I'd like to think cards like these were part of my reading, I can't say for sure.

I do know she explained that before I can actualize my path, I would have to be completely open to my mom, who sat behind me in this quaint broom closet—a typical demand of cartomancers who read for young teenagers is to have a parent in the room. The woman assured me that my mom would always offer support and that I should have faith in the act of being true to myself. I seized up. My stomach soured. She gave me a light-blue candle once my reading was finished, telling me to light it and ask for a smooth transition in owning my truth.

My mom and I sat in quiet on the way home once we left. She broke the silence, asking if I had anything I wanted to talk about. She reassured me that she would love me no matter what. I blurted out, "I'm bisexual, Mom."

"That's OK, honey," I can remember her say. "Momma always knew, and it's OK."

I came out to my friends earlier that year in high school. Now I'd come out to my mom. The tarot reading was in part the driving force for me to exit the closet. You could say, as far as literacy is concerned, the tarot was and has been a literacy sponsor in my life since that day. As I write this, a deck sits a few feet away, and I still consult its imagery routinely. Beginning with my coming-out story also brings into focus how closets can be filled with things that can help us queers decide when, where, and how to leave their confines. My closet, it just so happens, was literally represented by a broom closet. There were more things, more agents in my coming-out narrative, though.

Perhaps I would not have given much value to the tarot reading if it wasn't for the many trips to Kentucky backwoods and trailer parks that Mom and I took so many times. The car rides with my mom were part of my coming-out process, and by extension, the car was a safe enough space that allowed me to proclaim my sexuality that day. And it goes without stating that my mom is perhaps the most significant literacy sponsor in my life. She will tell you she didn't finish high school if you ask her. Her path to conventional literacy may be turbulent, but let me assure you, my mom is literate in ways most can't relate to. If it wasn't for her teaching me how to read the world, and in doing so, guaranteeing that I know how the world will misread me, then coming out that day wouldn't have been feasible; coming out takes plenty of actors, human and otherwise.

Furthermore, I don't think it's without reason to think of the phallic candle that was stored in the trailer closet as a literacy sponsor either. A mix of spirituality, desire, and illicit intent, the red cock hidden away in that trailer taught me early on that such non-Christian artifacts were to be tucked and stowed away. My desire for its shape was something to be concealed as well, even if it was unnamable at such a spry age. In fact, I realize now that I have never openly talked about the impact the candle made on me until now. The magical tool still serves a purpose. The cock candle has drawn me back in to assay how my sexual desire, my spiritual belief practices, and the way I come to interpret the world deeply coalesce on page, as a literacy scholar, as a queer Appalachian, and as a fifteen-year-old who came out because of tarot cards.

Most queer folx have coming-out stories even if their closets aren't full of tarot cards or priapic ritual supplies.[1] Usually coming out of the closet marks an ontological initiation into a life queerly lived. To make it plain, coming out of the closet is the act of disclosing nonheteronormative identity and/or sexual orientation. The idiom is oftentimes seen as a political act: "Since Stonewall, however, the 'closet' has become one of the most widely used metaphors for the evolution . . . of a gay or lesbian consciousness."[2] Eve Sedgwick, whose scrupulous theorizing of the closet is widely cited in queer theory, has noted that the closet was the "defining structure for gay oppression" in the twentieth century.[3] It's from Sedgwick's ideas that queer theorist Michael Warner aptly summarizes the function of the closet as "a set of assumptions in everyday life as well as in expert knowledge: assumptions about what goes without saying; what can be said without a breach of decorum; who shares the onus of disclosure; what can be known about a person's real nature through telltale signs, without his or her own awareness; and who will bear the consequences of speech and silence."[4]

The closet's pedigree isn't lost on literacy, composition, and rhetoric scholars, either. Notably, the first substantial instantiation of scholarship discussing coming out, the closet, and the writing classroom can be attributed to Malinowitz's *Textual Orientations*.[5] Malinowitz predicted over two decades ago that we would more frequently and in various ways have to grapple with coming out in the writing classroom: "Coming out is a speech act that, as the lesbian and gay movement grows and mass public discourse is increasingly infused with information about lesbian and gay existence, we can expect to see attempted more and more in our writing classroom."[6]

And she was correct. Scholars have since interrogated, for example, the representation of LGBT/queer peoples in texts used in writing classrooms and how queer texts can procure spaces of visibility.[7] The intersections of sexuality, technology, and the teaching of writing have garnered credence in the field as important places where the closet functions as well.[8]

There have been recent calls for more nuanced approaches to how we study and teach issues around coming out: "We must also remember that issues affecting LGBTQ students and teachers are wrapped up in queer sexuality and gender as they are with race, class, disability, citizenship, colonialism, and other factors. The issues that emerge from this scholarship need to be continually troubled along those additional lines. We must examine, for example, the role of reading and writing in coming out and sexual disclosures, specifically the shifting meanings of coming out across a diversity of LGBTQ experiences."[9]

Troubling such overlaps, I explore literacy matters of the closet, which is to say I ask questions that grapple with the social, systemic, and/or lived realities that accompany coming out but also contemplate what other *things* matter in coming out. Through engaging with one participant's coming-out story, I reimagine the closet as a metaphoric space of identity in addition to containing several unaccounted actants that are participatory with the process of coming out.

What would it mean to think of self-disclosure as an entangled, messy event not merely about a subject's identity alone or as a social phenomenon but one that involves a diversity of material actors? What would happen if we looked for *what* catalyzes the act of coming out rather than solely focusing on the coming out itself? How, in other words, can we animate the literacy act of declaring one's sexuality and/or gender as well as recognize the nonhuman actants involved with outing oneself? How can new materialist refigurations of agencies help us reimagine the way literacy emerges from being with the world or, in this case, the closet? More directly related to my participant pool, how does the physicality of Appalachia function in these narratives of coming out?

Following these lines of inquiry, I've titled this chapter "Matters of the Closet" as a deliberate attempt to rethink what *matter matters* in terms of the closet's metaphoric space. The dual meaning in *matters* opens a space for subverting meaning around the closet. If some-*thing* matters, it's important and has value. *The matters at hand* denotes priority and focus. Then there is the matter that makes up material. Such wordplay isn't my singular aim because I do realize and agree with the observation that "the belief that grammatical categories reflect the underlying structure of the world is a continuing seductive habit of mind worth questioning."[10] In lieu of being seduced by semantics, my point in this chapter looks to a literacy story I've collected from a queer Appalachian at length and with deep analysis in order to reconsider what matters in his literacy. More specifically, I am concerned with thinking through how coming-out stories not only are confined to discursive practices but rather are embodied enactments with a range of literacy sponsors that are not necessarily textual or, for that matter, human.

I closed the last chapter with the prospect of deploying metaphoric tracking in my research participants' stories as a model through which we can understand how literacy is caught in the flow of relationality with the nonhuman. If not obvious from its title, this chapter is concerned with the particular method of tracking literacy matters: metaphors that permit a glimpse into how being with objects and places in literacy is as equally important as the ability to read and write and all other acts of discernment. I've chosen the closet because, much like how other queer writers have reflected on the inanimate as critical to their queer lives, our relationship with objects *needs* to be queer if we are to better understand them outside of human exceptionalism.[11] The queer closet in this chapter is treated as a metaphor that contains multiple objects with their own agency and not merely a genre through which to read these participants' stories.

I see the closet as a material literacy metaphor in a few ways. To begin, the conventional closet is contingent on entry and departure from the same threshold, figuratively and literally. A closet sequesters what it contains. Matters of the closet frame this chapter because closets are full of stuff. We store things in a closet. The closet beckons us to hide our secrets, our failures: the dirty clothes we didn't wash before company arrives, the shoe obsession, nonaesthetic cleaning liquids and powdered agents used to keep the lived-in part of the house clean, a secret phallus-shaped candle, a place to give a tarot reading. Things get shoved into a closet not to be looked at. Yet they can also be wonderful places of chaos and mess. A closet can be a surreptitious place of queer awe.

In my analysis of literacy matters, I am adding to the copious amount of work that acknowledges the coming-out narrative as example par excellence in queer literacy work.[12] Coming-out narratives enable scholars to "unpack the layers of social, cultural, and ideological meaning and phenomena revealed and highlighted by the coming-out process."[13] Noting how "straights have the 'narrative luxury' of not having to consider their self-narration," it has been highlighted that coming out is "an act of rhetorical staging and performance, frequently on that is carefully crafted and narrated," whereas "coming-out stories seem almost always to be" personal narrative, centering around an individual's experience.[14] I want more from our scholarly acknowledgments about literacies of the closet. I want the things animating the closet to be given consideration along with the queer person who left or leaves its enclosure. I want the matters of the closet to be animated.

The closet reveals how our relationships with things are equally important in understanding their thing-power, or "the strange ability of ordinary, man-made items to exceed their status as objects and to manifest traces of independence or aliveness," and affects how we become and are literate.[15] On that note, we must account for the items in the closet. The closet isn't greater than the sum of its parts; each matter of the closet can hold as much value as the closet itself. The importance of the object isn't only about the thing unto itself, either, but instead its affiliation with the closet and the literacy act of coming out. Being open to receive such objects underlies animate literacies' federation with animacy theory: "Thinking and feeling critically about animacy encourages opening to the senses of the world, receptivity, vulnerability."[16] Animate literacies ask us to do the same with literacy. Matters of the closet ask us to do so queerly. Some closeted objects demand more attention than others. Some may recede to the background. Oftentimes one thing points to another, and their interactions push us out the door in unexpected ways.

Think of the tarot reading from my story earlier. Think of the table. Think of the cards. My being with those objects in that (actual and figurative) closet was just as important in my queer literacies as my self-disclosure. It's for this reason that in the following pages, I spend ample time with Justin's coming-out story. At the time of our interview, Justin was in his early thirties. And while he wasn't always drawn to English during his education, his interests in mathematics and arithmetic led to him teaching high school math. When Justin shared his story with me, he was finishing his master's in computation and had left high school teaching to pursue computer programming elsewhere. Justin grew up in the Appalachian region of southeast Ohio in a small rural town that ran along the Ohio River. He no longer lives in Appalachia but lives close enough to drive and visit his family when the occasion arises.

I go back into Justin's closet taking animate literacy with me and attempt to discover which objects existed with Justin that enabled and disenabled his coming out. I am looking for the actors in his stories that may or may not be central figures but nevertheless are enmeshed with the participant's coming-out narrative. The remainder of this chapter represents how I see literacy matters moving through storytelling, and as such, I spend a considerable amount of time with a single story to offer many ways of demonstrating animate literacies' theoretical application. Out of all the participants I interviewed, Justin's story stood out for having the most *things* in his closet. I look at the varieties of ways Justin's closet was actively shaping his world prior to his coming out. Then I explore how Justin's story illuminates an aspect often associated with the closet: death. From there I explore how closets contain things and how Justin's closet was filled with water heaters, scars, and hospital visits, among other things. Finally, I conclude this chapter with thinking about objects as they are taken out of the closet and what it may mean for objects outside the closet to work as literacy sponsors in the coming-out process.

Matters of Justin's Closet

Justin and I met when he was in a gay relationship with a close friend in 2015. I didn't know Justin was Appalachian like me until after he reached me on social media, willing to participate in my collecting of queer Appalachian stories. After deciding on a day and time, I interviewed Justin over the phone and recorded his interview on a voice recorder, later to be transcribed. It's important for context, as I will detail later, that Justin wasn't able to come out till he was twenty-five in large part due to a childhood accident that left 40 percent of his body covered in scars. He also has a twin gay brother. Otherwise, I have lightly edited the transcript to omit pauses and filler words for reading convenience. Scholars have made similar moves with their transcripts of participant interviews for ease of reading.[17] While my intention was not to edit for standardized American English like Sohn attempted to do with her participants, my editing sought to remove filler words that were nonstarters in terms of the storytelling. These include *um*, extra *like*s, *yeah*, *ya know*, and so on.

I initiated the interview by asking Justin how he identified. He told me he was "a cisgender male" and "100 percent homosexual," a factoid I felt silly inquiring about since these points were obvious from our friendship. However, during the length of the interview, I found out details of Justin's life that I hadn't known. Justin grew up in a family of six. While I knew that Justin has a twin who is also gay, I learned he had a younger and an older brother. He grew up with his mother and his father until they divorced when Justin was ten. Justin let me know early on in our conversation that he didn't come out till he was twenty-five: "I didn't come out [till] I was almost twenty-five. . . . I just never thought about my queerness or identity in any sort of sexual ways until I was twenty to twenty-three," he explained.

Even though Justin admits he didn't even "know what gay was," he realized he had same-sex desire from an early age. "I would grab the Sears catalog that we, for some weird reason, had in our bathroom," he explains, "and flip straight to the men's underwear section and start jerking off to it." Justin may not have been equipped with the sexual literacy to name his desire, if sexual literacy is limited only to the "knowledge complex that recognizes the significance of sexuality to self- and communal definition."[18] Justin's embodied desire made him literate, though. Justin was able to read the images of the men on display even if he wasn't "reading" alphabetic text. In this line of thinking, Justin's reading of the Sears catalog queerly fails to uphold conventional notions about what it means to be literate. As a nonhuman, nontextual (i.e., a text with words intended to be read) literacy sponsor, the Sears catalog animates how Justin became literate of his own desire, of bodies (his and other men's), and, later, of his sexual orientation. That is to say, Justin's sexual literacy emerges, at least in part, out of his interaction with the images of men in the catalog, his embodied urge "to start jerking off," and his desire for men.

When I asked Justin about when he was able to come out, his answer begins with him joining a college fraternity his junior year, where he "messed around with one guy." The way Justin puts it, "He got me kind of drunk—pretty drunk—over fall break. One thing led to another. I slept a night in his bed, and then he crawled up [into the bed]." This initial gay sexual encounter led to Justin living a double life. Between teaching Sunday school and running summer Bible study camps, "then on the weekends [going] to fool around with guys," Justin said, "I was still considering myself straight."

Justin took a year to come out completely, he told me: "I came out to my friends first. . . . I made it a birthday gift to myself. My birthday is in August, so I came out in about February of that year [to close friends]. I told everyone for my twenty-fifth birthday we cannot go out to get dinner and then go out afterwards . . . until I come out with everyone. I came out to my parents probably the Easter after my birthday. I thought I couldn't do it in person. I had to call my mom over the phone, but thankfully [my brother] had come out to them a couple years before me, so it wasn't that big of a deal."

Justin's plan to give a birthday gift to himself by coming out is an interesting metaphor to track here as a matter of his closet. A birthday gift, generally speaking, is arguably a metaphoric object that represents another year of one's life. The birthday gift exemplifies celebrating one's life, including the day of birth. Justin coming out, as I imagine it is for many queers who come out, marked a birth of a different sort.

Alongside the birth of his queer self, Justin made a comment that particularly stood out: "I was *so* naive. I had no idea what to expect, never had anything explained or never even explored those aspects of my life. I remember my mamaw passed away in February. This is 2009. The weekend before, I blacked out at a party and then woke up and was next to another man. She passed away the next weekend, and it was that pivotal moment in our family's life where, like, I finally had to be honest with myself."

He had *no* idea, *never* experienced, *never* explored those aspects of his life—those aspects I take to be those matters of living in the closet. The repetition of negatives underscored by blacking out—a temporary death of consciousness—and the death of his grandmother warrant pause as to how we can begin to think of the closet for Justin. The impetus "to be honest" with himself was catalyzed by death in Justin's narrative.

Arguably, the closet for Justin was a deadened place but one nevertheless still agential enough to propel Justin to disclosure. As not to forget, animacy at its core deals with liveliness and "seeks to trouble this binary of life and nonlife as it offers a different way to conceive of relationality and intersubjective exchange."[19] Animate literacies take seriously, too, the gradation of death: to what degree do absence, dying, and expiration function in our literate practices? To understand that Justin's closet was animated by his grandmother's death requires an explanation of how Justin sees his family. Later in our interview, when I asked about his relationship with his family now that he is out, Justin mentioned Appalachia for the first time and implicitly identified himself as being a part of "the very classic Appalachian family that doesn't talk about things." "Things" here isn't general for Justin; "things" is referring to his sexuality. He continued to explain, "I mean we're very quiet when it comes to family gatherings. They don't care [about his being gay]; we don't ever talk about things gay-related. They're very accepting of us [i.e., Justin and his gay twin brother]." Justin's family avoiding anything "gay-related" while being "very accepting" of Justin and his lifestyle could be perceived as contradictory, especially when queer politics oftentimes relies on a *we're here, we're queer* mentality. I think this contradiction can exist because family takes on queerer meaning in Appalachia.

For instance, in her recent work, Appalachian rhetorician Amanda Hayes notes how Appalachian rhetoric's "reliance on place and family are not only as socially important concepts (which they are), but also on an implicit understanding that these are sources of knowledge on which to build one's process of thinking and identity-building."[20] Appalachia as an actual place, not mere social category, is actively involved with the formation of how Appalachians think and how Appalachians identify. What's more, "place," she writes, "can be family. Family can be place."[21] Hayes's chiasmatic articulation about family and place reveals how place matters for Appalachians, an arguably queer perspective. It is queer first because it exposes place as agential in Appalachia; the land has the power to form familial relations and kinships, leaving room for different kinships and different closets to emerge much like the possibilities that lie in queer kin-making. Furthermore, by claiming that place can be family, the power of Appalachian place transgresses sanguine genealogies, subverting normative familial structures by including the inanimate kin of the landscape. It's a very queer notion to entertain that, like queers who choose their families, the land via an Appalachian rhetorical lens can also choose its family. The Appalachian Mountains are a queer family member.

Since Appalachian families can be potentially viewed as queer because of their incorporation of the mountains as kin, it's important to acknowledge that Justin's grandmother dying potentially signifies his relationship to the mountains and his being Appalachian. He can articulate his queerness once he experiences loss and finds himself away at college, outside the Appalachian region. Justin's deliberation to come out to everyone as a gift to himself was marked by the death of his grandmother, demonstrating how closets can be queer places, teetering between life and death. For Justin, his coming out was both a moment of celebrating his natal birth and the birth of his queer self while simultaneously acknowledging how the death of his grandmother led to killing off the parts of his life where he could no longer be honest with himself. The argument could be made that his grandmother was a competing sponsor of literacy, meaning she inhibited his coming out.[22] Justin never indicated that it was particularly his grandma who prevented him from coming out. It was what her death represented that, perhaps, was the reason he couldn't be honest with himself: his relationship to place and family. In this way, an animate literacy sponsor that works to inhibit literacy could just as well be the *relations* among place and the sponsored and the familial relationships.

In fact, speaking of his family, Justin did not say much about the process of his brother's coming out, which Justin explains little about besides it "happening his [brother's] freshman year." What I do find striking here is the matter of proximity of Justin's closet to his family and his parents back home. Justin's reluctance to coming out in person to his parents calls into question how locality can shift the closet's agency. It needs to be considered, then, how closets gain or lose power in proximity to where they are when someone is still closeted. Justin's closet loses the capacity to hold him when he is farther from his family of origin. Justin's coming out over the phone read through a conventional literacy lens may focus on only Justin's agency: Justin was more willing to come out when he wasn't home, and so it's a matter of Justin's agency. But to end at that point would elide the matters of Justin's closet. We should also ask how the closet as a thing changes in proximity to place—it wasn't just that Justin felt safer or felt it easier to come out not face to face with his parents, but it was *also that he was in a different place*. Agency doesn't solely lie in Justin's possession here but with a conglomeration of literacy sponsors: the death of his grandmother, the proximity of his closet, the clandestine hookups, the denial, the phone in his hand. All these factors were equally important in the lead-up to and the act of self-disclosure for Justin, as, I'm venturing to say, is the case for all us queers and our closets.

The Things in Justin's Closet

Ask just about anyone who has come out about their process, and they can tell you where and when they did, perhaps even how they still must out themselves in various contexts and settings. Justin couldn't come out earlier in his life in part because of his relationship to his body. Justin explained he was not able to think about his sexuality till his early twenties, and he had good reason.

There's no denying that Justin's first twenty years were shaped by his relationship to his body because they were spent dealing with the scars left by a severe burn from bath water. He explains, "It's taken me a long time, even this year being in therapy, to realize I'm allowed to be comfortable with myself." Justin detailed how being five feet and weighing 255 pounds at the end of his junior year of high school made matters worse: "I just made the decision because it was the only way I figured I knew how to lose weight.... It started with stop drinking pop," he continued, "and then it turned into not eating at all, and I dropped ninety pounds in one year." Justin confesses, "I went anorexic and then bulimic my entire senior year." Struggling with eating disorders and his weight along with the myriad of complications that resulted from the burns left Justin thinking, "I sure as hell won't be desirable... why even try?" Moreover, it was his scars "that was a major thing that delayed [his] sexual exploration."

Earlier on in our interview, he told me the tragic story about what occurred to him as a toddler:

> So I have third-degree burns on almost 40 percent of my body. It's from halfway up my butt then down to my feet. . . . I would go through surgeries every year, every other year till I was about fourteen or fifteen and then have one every few years after that. . . .
> It was an accident. My dad was home with me and [Justin's twin brother]. It was about ten in the morning . . . we had a routine, and I don't exactly know how it would happen, sometimes one of us would have a bath, then the other, sometimes together. I was fifteen months old. Dad had [my brother] in one room, and then I just ran into the bathroom, just like a toddler would do, then jumped in the bathtub, knelt on both my knees, and then turned the hot water faucet on. This is in December of 1985, and hot water heaters then would produce hot water so much faster than they do today. There were not as many regulations. . . . So it only took five seconds to get scalding hot water to come out, and then about ten seconds later, I had 35–40 percent of my body burned.

Thinking through the closet as the framework in this chapter, it's important to be mindful that bodies are in closets as well. New materialist perspectives wouldn't limit bodies exclusive to human domain. They would not demarcate the human body as a closed-off, distinct entity either. By way of this thinking, I'd like to suggest that the body itself, apart from our awareness of it, can act as a literacy sponsor: "That is, human bodies, like all other bodies, are not entities with inherent boundaries and properties but phenomena that acquire specific boundaries and properties through the open-ended dynamics of intra-activity. Humans are part of the world-body space in its dynamic structuration."[23]

Justin's story of how he was burned read through this argument offers insight as to how his body entered the closet. Understanding that "it is thus not enough to say that we are 'embodied.' We are, rather, *an array of bodies*," it serves to spend time with how boiling water, water heaters, and Justin's scars form an assemblage shaping his body, able to produce a closet deep enough that he wasn't able to find his way out till his mid-twenties.[24] When Justin explained that water heaters weren't "regulated the way they are today," I was curious to discover the history of their regulation.

Two years prior to Justin being burned in 1983, Washington was the first state to pass legislation that "recognizes that unnecessarily hot tap or bath water creates an extreme risk of severe burns, especially among the elderly, children, and retarded persons."[25] Problematic language notwithstanding, the state law resulted from three years of lobbying and the advocacy from pediatricians on behalf of children and the frequent burns they experienced from too hot bathwater.[26] Afterward, states began to adopt various plumbing codes capping water temperatures as they see fit for residential water heaters—federal precedent only required a warning on the water heater detailing that boiling water can cause serious, potentially fatal burns. Over the next seven years, the power of federal regulation in water heater installation would only reach hospitals and medical facilities, uniform standards for disabled access in public buildings, and prisons and jails.[27] It wouldn't be until 1997 that Ohio state law would adhere to a plumbing code mandating an anti-scald valve on all residential water heaters, which shut off water flow over 120°F.[28]

Water heater legislation and regulation were underway as fifteen-month-old Justin spent the year after being burned undergoing eight surgeries. The doctors "removed tissue and started the skin-grafting process," he said, and "twenty years after that, it was a mixture of physical therapy and skin-graft surgeries." If agency is "an enactment, not something that someone or something has," we cannot completely account for the specific agents that caused Justin to be burned.[29] Put another way, animate literacies aren't necessarily asking whose actions were the cause of Justin's burns.

Animate literacies' acknowledgment of agency as existing with nonhumans—in this case, the water heater—"means that accountability requires much more attentiveness to existing power asymmetries."[30] Power is understood here not as "an external force that acts on a subject" but power as the reiterative enactments between human and nonhumans that become sedimented over time.[31] The water heater, both for Justin personally and independent from his story, serves to demonstrate how nonhuman agents can possess thing-power. The water heater's thing-power being caught up in regulatory systems exhibits how nonhumans can sweep us up in strange currents of relations. Moreover, it isn't only the relationality of actors that is important to animate literacies but the meaning-making that emerges from the performances, the sign systems, and the sensate necessary to navigate such interconnections.

Justin's story can help clarify my point. Picking up where he left off earlier, "My dad's deaf, and so he didn't necessarily hear it at first, and then he came running in and had to wrap me up in the towel and take me to the neighbors' house so they could call 911."

Looking back, I realize Justin never explained if his dad had access to a Teletypewriter, sometimes referred to as a TTY, and I was so intent on listening that I didn't think to ask. Regardless of this fact, I must carefully consider embodiment's role in how Justin creates meaning: his own embodiment from being scarred, his dad's nonnormative embodiment in an immediate environment that didn't enable him to directly contact 911 for help, proximity of Justin's neighbors. As a result, Justin's retelling of his story is somatically constitutive. Justin is now literate of things like water heaters in ways others aren't but also of skin grafts, physical therapies, and surgeries. Acknowledging Justin's animate literacies as founded in the sensate is to simultaneously recognize that the water heater's thing-power lies in its reiterative encounters with humans. The intersections of the regulatory power set in motion by the lobbying and protests of pediatricians on behalf of children on the other side of the continental United States linger behind Justin's story.

Alison Kafer's insights on the body in her theorizing of crip theory can help explain how closeted objects function as literacy sponsors and actants in queer literacy practices. Crip theory proposes that disability and, by proxy, "crip"-ness are cultural orderings used to uphold systemic structures of heteronormativity and able-bodiedness or compulsory able-bodiedness. Crip theory, in several ways, relies on queer theory's destabilization of normalized sexualities and genders in order to claim that cripness undermines social forms that purport bodies should *be* only one way and, moreover, should be "able" in particular ways.[32]

Kafer builds from these arguments and offers another crip framework that she calls the *political/relational* model. "Under a political/relational model of disability," she writes, "the problem of disability is located in inaccessible buildings, discriminatory attitudes, and ideological systems that attribute normalcy and deviance to particular minds and bodies."[33] Situating Kafer's argument next to my ongoing invocation of new materialist agency, I don't think we should ignore that objects have a relational and political, and thus potentially queer, role to play in how we come to understand bodies and their impact in literacy. This becomes especially true when we take into account the multitude of bodies, objects, and places that closets contain. For Justin, the water heater wasn't only a literacy sponsor by its impact on his embodiment, but its thing-power was also brought into relief by the political structures that surround it.

Recall that litigation passed on regulating water heaters because of the bodies that unregulated water heaters were affecting on a continual basis. Water heaters were a particular threat to "the elderly, children, and retarded persons." Read through a crip lens, the power of the water heater jeopardized the nonnormalized body. This law makes room "to trace the ways in which compulsory able-bodiedness/able-mindedness and compulsory heterosexuality intertwine in the service of normativity."[34] The potential for damaging the body that the unregulated water heater possessed was a threat to those bodies deemed not normal—the water heater was a queer/crip object because of its potential to disfigure and make more queer those bodies already deemed other. For Justin, the water heater initially limited his understanding of his own queerness—his scarred embodiment occluded his queer desires and identity.

Part of the reason he thinks it's taken him till his thirties to accept his body and his identity as queer is due to the "Appalachian mentality," where you just "deal with" the "adversity in your life. You can't improve [the situation], so you just have to play the cards you're dealt." Not to diminish Justin's point of view nor his lived experience as being Appalachian, but this stereotyping of the Appalachian mentality has been critiqued by scholars. The homogenizing cultural narrative that Appalachians are isolationists residing in the mountains who aim to keep outsiders out is bolstered by a parallel narrative that Appalachians don't want to better themselves because there's no sense in it, a point that Justin seems to regard as true.[35] I'm not interested in negotiating existing scholarship with Justin's perspective; in fact, I find the irreconcilability even more productive in supporting my arguments in chapter 2 on Appalachia as a queer place. What I'd like to think through, rather, are the ways Appalachia acts in concert with the water heater in Justin's closet.

I argue that Justin's perception of Appalachia and the scholarly critique are both contradictory and true from the viewpoint of animate literacies' agential understanding of place. For instance, Justin told me, after I asked him how his family navigated the years of surgeries with a family of six, "So a lot of our family lived in the same town. . . . Thankfully visits for just one day [when] we'd go to [the hospital]; it'd be a day trip if we went for a checkup. If I was in for a surgery, my three brothers would stay with our mamaw and papaw or stay with an aunt or uncle."

The meaningful relationships that enabled Justin to continue his surgeries were not merely social if we bear in mind that animate literacies flow through place. Place provided material resources, and his family functioned as sponsors of his queer literacy. Place shaped and funneled Justin's personal and familial relationships. Living close to family and neighbors allowed Justin to make meaning in the world through his body. Adding to this, it's critical not to lose sight that place is also tangled in the water heater's thing-power via lack of regulation because Justin's burns were created in Appalachia Ohio, not West Coast Washington, permanently affecting Justin's relationship to his body. So when I say that scholarly critiques of narratives about Appalachia can be suspended in a queer web of agential factors for Justin's literacies, I mean animate literacies embrace contradictions and moments of misfiring insofar as academic literacy practices are concerned. Justin's story reveals how physical place and the objects that participate therein are constitutive in the formation of animate literacy practices.

Justin's literacy narrative upholds my view of literacy as an exchange of forces emanating from a combination of sign systems, performances, and the sensate. While it may be the case that I focus less on how literacy emanates from sign systems for Justin, with the legislation being the most apt example, I think it is apparent how the synesthetic and the performative shape Justin's literacies. How he read his body through sensational means, how he performed in his body, how the water heater accident was somatic and lasting—all these sensations and performances structured the closet around Justin. The literacy matters involved with closet-building act as a metaphor we can track to understand that literacy isn't only a matter of reading and writing but of queer world-making.

A Closet's Worth

"Our metaphors, our tropes, our analogies," Kafer proclaims, "all have histories, all have consequences."[36] The onus of this chapter has been the metaphor of the closet as an animated literacy sponsor that contains tangible, physical bodies and objects. Furthermore, through examining the metaphor of the closet up close, we can begin to understand how the bodies and objects in them have their own agency that underscore the literacy act of proclaiming one's queerness. By highlighting how place is also a critical factor in the construction of closets, it has been my aim to argue that closets are enlivened by the ability to move in space. They are alive, too, by their ability to catalyze death and inanimacy into action. Kafer states that our metaphors—in this case, metaphors that contain matters of literacy—carry with them responsibility to critique their histories and implications of use. By spending time with the metaphor and literacy act of coming out of the closet, so readily accepted in literacy scholarship, I show how metaphors of matter work to animate our understanding and incorporation of the nonhuman into our expertise.

To stake these claims, I have focused solely on a single story from the many hours of my story collecting to demonstrate there are numerous ways of engaging matters of literacy. To list and gloss over Justin's closet to make room for other participants' closets would have been a disservice to Justin and all that his closet entails. To quickly sort through Justin's closet would have also been irresponsible of me on the behalf of my reader; spending an entire chapter to explore Justin's closet enabled me to show how animate literacies can be analyzed and discovered in storytelling. I'm left wondering: What happens to the objects in our closets once we decided to come out? What happens to the objects that are or were shut away? I'd like to conclude with rethinking the use of the closet as a literacy sponsor once the coming out is over. Justin's story led me to ask these questions, and it is his story that I'd like to close with analyzing.

Toward the end of our interview, Justin elucidated that it was only in his thirties that he could feel comfortable being gay and being scarred: "I'm allowed to show myself to other people and not be ashamed of it." While Justin doesn't expand how he shows himself, I would venture to say that Justin is discussing the history of his closet that's rendered visible on his body through his scarring. This is a safe assumption because Justin tells me about a significant Pride event he attended in 2017: "Even if it's something as simple as last Pride . . . at last year's Pride, it was the first time I had ever worn shorts to Pride. I've only been to a few [Prides], but it's a fucking hundred degrees outside. And I remember being like, 'Oh my god, [wearing pants and long sleeves] is miserable.' So I said fuck it. I'm wearing a cut-off shirt and shorts, and it was glorious."

Pride is celebrated across the United States during June to remember the Stonewall riots that occurred on June 28, 1969, which set in motion the subsequent gay rights movement. Most Prides are held outdoors and involve parades in public streets; drag shows are performed in outside auditoriums or on erected stages. June can certainly come with temperatures reaching a "fucking hundred degrees." Justin's ability to read the world, and the world that read his body as different—arguably queer, even within the queer community—cumulates in a single act of wearing shorts.

Shorts. Think about wearing shorts. What does it mean to consider wearing shorts when your legs or body may be read by the world as somehow unacceptable? For some, shorts may not mean much more than reprieve from the hot months. For Justin, even after coming out, the matters of his closet are still shaping how the world comes to interact with his body and his own understanding of his queerness. By wearing a sleeveless shirt and a pair of shorts (which I'd like to imagine him choosing from his closet at the time), without uttering a word, Justin declares his queerness. He uses his closet's matters to disclose his queer sexuality by attending a Pride event; he queers his relationship to his body by refusing its concealment—by visibly showing his scars that got in the way of his queerness to begin with. Yet the shorts have the agency to do so—the shorts *and* the scars *and* the water heater *and* the Sears catalog *and, and, and.* When I ask what we are to do after the literacy act of coming out is over, I think Justin can teach us a few things: closets don't disappear once queers exit them. Closets can pull us back in. They exist in our literacies to animate the past, reminding us of when we sought new life as queers killing off our silence. They also teach us that everyone's closets can hold multitudes. Justin's closet wasn't full of tarot cards or cock candles; his closet contained water heaters and hospital visits and scars. Finally, Justin's closet reveals how the matters of the closet can follow up, the contents brushing up against our bodies and literacies. The shorts in his closet influenced Justin years after he had come out. Closets can remind us that how we choose to be with nonhumans matters in how we discern the world while revealing that the world around us can easily build closets around us without our doing.

4

Queer Affinities

Originally, when setting out to do this project, I planned to organize the chapters by each area of the participants' lives that I inquired about during the interview process—trauma, body, place, and spirituality (see interview questions in the appendix). However, my work had plans of its own and set me down another path. I came to realize how my theory of animate literacies was animating my own writing. For this reason, in the previous chapter, by looking at objects via the literacy matters of Justin's closet, I aimed to demonstrate how such nonhumans are caught up in the flow of literacy *emanating from a combination of sign systems, performances, and the sensate.* Furthermore, in accordance with my assertion that literacy *flows through and in particular places,* Appalachia has funneled the flow of this entire manuscript. I am left with the task of elucidating and unpacking the remaining piece of my definition of literacy: how literacy may be understood as an *exchange of forces.*

To do so requires examining up close what I mean by *force* and what it means to exchange. I am not limiting exchange to its transactional sense. That is, an exchange in the way I see working in literacy isn't for mere purpose of gaining one thing for another as you would, say, trade money for goods—it isn't always about profit for animating literacy. My use of *exchange* rests on the meaning of its core word, *change.* You can change your behavior, change the load of laundry, change a diaper, carry change in your pocket. Through the lens of animacies theory, change's agency rests in the ability to affect. Even as an object, pocket change still causes things to happen. What's more, with regard to how literacy flows through places, I find it coincidental the word may have some far distant relation to Appalachia's Irish history: "from Old French *changier* 'to change, alter; exchange, switch,' from Late Latin *cambiare* 'to barter, exchange,' extended form of Latin *cambire* 'to exchange, barter,' a word of Celtic origin, from PIE (Proto-Indo-European) root **kemb-* 'to bend, crook' (with a sense evolution perhaps from 'to turn' to 'to change,' to 'to barter'); cognate with Old Irish *camm* 'crooked, curved'; Middle Irish *cimb* 'tribute,' *cimbid* 'prisoner.'"[1]

An exchange, as I use it to define animate literacies, is the bending and crooked forces that ultimately *effect change, creating new ways of being with and meaning-making*. The Irish roots may not have been an intentional connection I made from the beginning, but I can't ignore how even in my framing of this project, I am still finding connections to Appalachia. If sexualities are queer because they "are seen as odd, bent, twisted," then I can't help but see literacy as an exchange of forces being queer by way of its etymological origins.[2] *Exchange* seems suitable enough a term to think of literacy as an ongoing movement of forces.

Literacy affects are deployed in our literacy practices by demonstrating ways of being affected and how we potentially affect others. Where my discussion of literacy matters in the last chapter pointed to things, coherent enough to exist on their own in participants' storytelling, my discussion of literacy affects points to states of being. Literacy affects bear witness to how an exchange of forces can bend meaning, make crooked sense, and queer relationality. Recall that my method of discovering animate literacies relies on tracking specific types of metaphors in our storytelling and that literacy affects are metaphors that deal with how subjectivity is contained within literacy practices. The subjective *I* is a clear first indication that a metaphor may have the potential to be considered a literacy affect. The metaphors that make up literacy affects rely on verbiage that indicates states rather than action or processes or, in linguistics terminology, stative verbs. That being said, I don't want to become too mired in linguistics and lose sight of how matters of nonhuman agency, affective states, and queerness underscore animate literacies altogether. In fact, in tracking metaphors, literacy matters and literacy affects oftentimes overlap.

I, too, "equate affect with materiality" when considering all actors' capacity to affect, but to condense the two into a single theoretical framework with regard to literacy would be a mistake.[3] If we are to bring new materialism and posthumanist ethics into our literacy research, then we have to (1) attend to the fact that there are nonhumans that participate in literacies and have strategies to identify them; (2) consequently, to see that literacy emerges from an exchange of forces, it's essential to locate moments in literacy practices that expose various actants' capacity *to affect* one another for change to occur. This chapter takes the latter as its main goal.

It is necessary to delineate the meaning of *affect*. What's more, it's critical to understand the relationship and slippage between the terms *affect* and *emotion* since they, in many ways, can be strikingly similar, even interchangeable, yet can philosophically differ. Because I'm interested in the affects of various forces between an assemblage of actors in literacy, I've chosen to title this "Queer Affinities" and have not included the word *affect* in the title for a particular reason. While *affect* and *affinity* may not share etymological roots, they still, as I see it, exist in an orbit of one another. *Affect*, from the Latin *ad*, "to," and *facere* or *factus*, "to make, do," in a literal translation means "to do to." Affinity, on the other hand, is a cognate of *affinitas*, from *affinis*, directly translated as "bordering on." Affinities could be thought of as identifiable contact zones between affects. To put it another way, affinities are the formation of affects when they brush up against bodies. If you have an affinity for someone or something, you are inclined to be affected by such actants. In a generic sense, for instance, you can say that you have an affinity for science-fiction novels or for cheap smut. But animate literacies seek out queer affinities that don't necessarily fit into convention.

This chapter, which is examining literacy affects, is titled "Queer Affinities" because it points to how affects leave their mark on queers through literacy. I am interested in how queer relationships among all actors congeal through literacy practices. That is, this chapter is concerned with identifying the lasting, queer affinities among individuals, bodies, nonhumans, and the land that form via literacy practices. With each story, I begin with moments of participants' writing, reading, and other acts of literacy to demonstrate how participants' affective states linger past the page, forming queer affections between the storyteller and others. I look to four participants' stories to demonstrate such queer affiliations.

While I go into detail for each story in the second half of this chapter, I'll quickly highlight the queer storytellers' information here. I begin with Lexi's story. Lexi is a mother, an ex-wife, and a recovering drug addict. She identifies as bisexual and lives in central West Virginia. The second story belongs to Elizabeth. Elizabeth was born in Kentucky, but as an infant, her parents quickly moved her to Tennessee, where she remained till after graduate school. She identifies as bisexual and lives with her trans partner in rural New York. Macy's story comes next. Macy grew up in southern Ohio, on the banks of the Ohio River. She identifies as a bi- and pansexual cisgender woman. Currently, Macy is finishing her bachelor's degree at a Midwestern university in Ohio. Finally, the last story belongs to Lara. Lara came to live in southeast Kentucky as a teenager from New Mexico. She is bisexual and attending an Appalachian private college in Kentucky.

When I say that each story begins with typical literacy practices, I mean journaling, writing, interacting on social media, reading novels, and conducting research. Lara's and Macy's stories also include sexual literacy practices.[4] These involve teaching others about sexuality, safe-sex practices, and writing and revising policies on campus that affect bathroom access for trans students. Also, there are commonalities among these storytellers: they all identify as cisgender women; all four identify as bisexual (though Macy, who identifies as pansexual, uses the term *bisexual* only in certain contexts, but more on this later); not counting Lexi, the three other participants experienced living outside of Appalachia; excluding Elizabeth, the other three discuss feeling as though their bisexuality is not taken seriously or discounted; all four perceive of evangelical Christianity in Appalachia as harmful either to their own relationship with the church and religion or to the queer community at large, sometimes even both.

These four participants' stories are unique because their reading and writing practices affect their understanding of self, place, and community. Community, as I'm using it here, varies for each participant but is always underscored by their relationship to others. In a number of ways, the local places where the participants practice their literacies become animated and affect their understanding of self. In other words, the relationship between self and place is affected and mediated through their literacy practices. The subtle details in each story begin to stitch together a clearer picture of animate literacies' expansion and reformation of literacy as an ongoing exchange of forces, pushing actors together and apart. Through paying attention to the lasting affinities that are generated from reading, writing, and other literacy practices, it becomes easier to see how literacy is alive, energic, and forceful with the capacity to affect not only how one reads and writes but also how actors relate to and within the world.

Queerly Affected

Emotions and affects are connected but still distinct conceptions. It's been noted that "an emotion is a subjective content, the sociolinguistic fixing of the quality of an experience which is from that point onward defined as personal."[5] In other words, emotions are possessed by an individual. *I am sad.* Sadness belongs to the subject in this statement. Affect speaks to something else: "affect is synesthetic, implying a participation of the senses in each other: the measure of a living thing's potential interactions is its ability to transform the effects of one sensory mode into those of another."[6] Emotions attempt to capture those moments of sensory participation.

Affect can be understood as "an ability to affect and a susceptibility to be affected," whereas an "emotion or feeling is a recognized affect."[7] In this way of thinking, it follows that affects precede emotion. Emerging from these ideas, affect theory grew to elucidate and expand affect's reach as being "synonymous with force or forces of encounter" and, in further detail, "affect's always immanent capacity for extending further still: both into and out of the interstices of the inorganic and the non-living, the intracellular divulgences of sinew, tissue, gut economies, and the vaporous evanescences of the incorporeal."[8] Affect includes the potentiality of the space around and in us. There is a myriad of force relations; "affect as potential" equals "a body's capacity to affect and be affected."[9] The feeling that's left after being affected or affecting another we come to call *emotions.*

Emotions, since they are personal and nameable, have been theorized as well. Notably, the psychologist and science reporter Daniel Goleman developed an influential (though also problematic) theory of emotions and was quickly circulated in popular self-help discourse. He argues that emotions are as critical in thinking about intelligence as mental cognition, noting, "Emotional life is a domain that, as surely as math or reading, can be handled with greater or lesser skill, and requires its unique set of competencies."[10] Goleman's neologism of emotional intelligence is widely used still as "a meta-ability, determining how well we can use whatever other skills we have including raw intellect."[11] It isn't outside the realm of reason to see parallels between the ability-based model of literacy and Goleman's definition of emotional intelligence. Because of this, other scholars have built on this framework, leading to the concept of emotional literacy as an "ability to understand and manage emotions resourcefully, to communicate effectively, and to self-coach [which] are essential for all of us."[12] Emotional literacy is distinct from emotional intelligence in that the latter "is the characteristic, the personality dynamic or the potential, that can be nurtured and developed in a person," and the former "is the constellations of understandings, skills, and strategies that a person can develop and nurture from infancy through his or her entire lifetime."[13]

Conceptually, emotional literacy and emotional intelligence demonstrate how these lexical variations are intimately reliant on individualization and are important in thinking about how literacy is always linked to an individual's ability. The capacity to understand one's emotive life is linked to learning how to be emotionally literate. One example stands out: learning how to grapple with one's emotional states and what situations trigger those emotions has increasingly played a role in the mental health of students in primary and secondary education.[14] However, I think it serves to question what limitations accompany emotional literacy when we restrict emotions to merely a personal matter. Mark Amsler offers alternative perspectives of literacy in terms of affect theory in his book *Affective Literacies: Writing and Multilingualism in the Late Middle Ages*. Drawing from medieval historiography, literary studies, and the New Literacy Studies movement, Amsler defines affective literacies as "a range of emotional, spiritual, physiological, somatic responses readers have when reading or perceiving a text."[15] The assortment of responses he describes relies on three suppositions: the first being that there must exist a text to provide a response, second that the reader is literate enough in the particular type of text to have a response, and finally that affective literacies are still firmly situated within the domain of human experience. Although I found Amsler's connection of literacy and affect useful, Amsler is still placing center to affective literacies the human exceptionalism that I've critiqued. My theoretical view of affect differs from Amsler's because it doesn't rely solely on the affective states experienced while reading a book. Nor does animate literacies presume that to be affectively literate requires reading and writing in the traditional sense. After all, it's estimated that human communication is primarily nonverbal; we can read each other's bodies and be affected too.[16]

I'd like to think that a posthuman, new materialist perspective can broaden affect's role in literacy studies: the "posthuman subject finds herself immersed in a network of vital relations, not autonomous at all, yet autopoietic, reproducing and transforming in relation to assemblages of which she is part."[17] Since "posthuman literacy researchers recognize that we are part of the ongoing activity of life," literacy affects don't limit emotions to merely something one possesses or some phenomenologically individual experience.[18] My theory of animate literacies treats affects and emotions—in their own right—as separate pseudo-entities that render relationality visible in our stories.[19] Emotion "best evokes the potential to enact and construct, name and define, become and undo—to perform meanings and to stand as a marker for meanings that get performed," notably because "bodies and emotions are not only enacted in writing but also imbued in how we come to writing."[20]

Emotions and affect overlap because "emotions do something besides express individuals' feelings, usually thought of as internal states; emotions function as the adhesive that aligns certain bodies together and binds a person/position/role to an affective state."[21] To put it another way, "emotions are something we do rather than something we have."[22] Because emotions are a doing, as literacy scholar Micciche argues, and I'm inclined to agree, they're inseparable from the writing process: "Writing involves everything you do, everything you encounter, everything you are when making sense of the world through language. Writing is contaminated, made possible by a mingling of forces and energies in diverse, often distributed environments. Writing is defined, ultimately, by its radical *withness*."[23]

There's that word again: *with*. The exchange of forces, which animate literacies offer to broaden literacy's domain of expertise, relies on being with others, as Micciche is pointing to here. To say that writing is contaminated also gestures toward my queer application of affect in animate literacies.

Affects have the potential to become queer when their effects fail to reproduce acceptable, normative emotive, or embodied states. If animacy hierarchies are "ontologies of affect," we must account for how affects order bodies as acceptable or not.[24] Sara Ahmed's "affective economies" may be helpful, where she sees the object-subject relationship bound together by affects. For Ahmed, "emotions involve subjects and objects, but without residing positively within them."[25] Ahmed claims that "emotions are relational: they involve (re)actions or relations of towardness or awayness" with particular objects.[26] The "words for feeling, and objects of feeling, circulate and generate effects," she also writes; "they move, stick, and slide," and we "move, stick and slide with them."[27] Queer feelings become "'affected' by the repetition of the scripts they fail to reproduce, and this 'affect' is also a sign of what queer can do, of how it can work by working on the (hetero)normative."[28] Queer affects, as I see them being deployed in a theory of animate literacies, ask: How can affects queer our understanding of literacy, and how are queers affected by literacies? How can the feelings of queers offer insight into literacy practices that challenge meaning-making?

Through Lexi's, Elizabeth's, Macy's, and Lara's stories, my aim is not necessarily to answer these questions but point out the lasting affects of literacy for these participants. Their narratives don't speak for all queers, and as you'll see, even sometimes their experiences are in tension with one another. When I read through and listen back to their stories, I'm reminded that one of the queerest things we can do is meditate on irresoluteness. Not finding any solid answers in storytelling is, in its own way, a literacy affect because it asks us to sit with their potential to trouble our understanding of literacy. I hope as you read the following stories, you, too, will find that "staying with the trouble requires learning to be truly present" with the "myriad unfinished configurations of places, times, matters, meanings."[29] I want to offer a word of warning: the stories in this chapter deal with sensitive issues—like molestation, rape, drug use, strong religious condemnation—and some details may be challenging to read.

Lexi's Story: Affective Research

Trigger Warning: This Story Contains Molestation and Drug Use

Lexi had a harrowing story to tell. Her interview has haunted me since this research began because of its difficult content. When I interviewed Lexi in the spring of 2018, she was twenty-eight years old. Lexi identifies as a bisexual woman, and being bisexual in her experience has left her at times feeling that "people don't necessarily take seriously" her attraction to women and men. She refers to herself as an addict and had been sober since New Year's at the time of our meeting. She is also a mother. The father of her son is now her ex-husband after a five-year relationship, with the last year spent being married. Until she started dating women, she had never experienced any trauma with regard to her sexuality, "never really had any issues" when she was only dating men. "It was terrible," she told me. Her first girlfriend "had a lot going on." To add insult to injury, she explains this first same-sex relationship didn't sit well with her son's father:

> My ex-husband called CPS [Child Protective Services] on me because I was being with a woman. It didn't go anywhere, of course. He didn't like the environment that [her son] was being raised in. . . . He showed his true colors around [her gay friend]. He wasn't OK

with gays. He didn't want his son to be around them. And once I started to date girls, he was just not happy about the situation he [her son] was being raised in, which I thought was absolutely beautiful. [Her son] had a tough time for a second because he was used to the man-woman [relationship], but after a little while, he ended up coming around.

She revealed these details to me in the first ten minutes. As Lexi continued narrating during our interview, I grew increasingly aware that her life and literacy practices were stitched together by traumatic events.

When I asked her what trauma may look like outside the relationship to her sexuality, her answers were arresting. I quote at length here in order to grasp the full breadth and gravity of Lexi's experience:

That trauma looks like a young girl being taken advantage of when she was twelve by a close family member. My father always used drugs his whole life. There was an instance when I was young and I was sleeping in his bed, and he didn't know it was me. He started rubbing on my body, above [my] clothes, but at that moment, my whole life changed. That's when my childhood went away, when my whole self changed. I started getting angry. I didn't tell anyone except my best friend, and she went to my mom. I dealt with my whole family not believing me. I got in trouble for it, but my dad didn't get in trouble for it. I'm glad he didn't get in trouble for it because I love him. . . . I've been raised around drug addiction all throughout my family. My grandmother and father were in recovery, so I never saw them using. My father was in prison for fourteen years of my life. He was the main reason I knew I was going to try everything [every drug], every one, whatever was placed in front of me. I wanted

> to do what I consider research because I wanted to understand what took my dad from me. 'Cause he would get out of prison, and he'd be good, he'd be my dad. And then within so long he would have a girlfriend. Shortly after that, I wouldn't see him anymore. I didn't understand why it would happen. So I wanted to understand why it took my dad. I wanted to know what mind-altering substances do. He'd tell me not to do it. I'd want to do it more. I achieved everything I wanted to achieve.

I ask her when she said she "had to try every one" if she meant drugs. She confirmed, yes, she's "done every drug." "Being an addict," as she refers to herself throughout the interview many times, is a theme underlying Lexi's narrative. Drugs are everywhere. Lexi tells me that we wouldn't have to walk far in the West Virginian town where we sat during her interview to buy any. In fact, at the time of the interview, West Virginia led the country with the most overdoses from drugs, particularly meth and opiates.[30] When Lexi explained the reasons she has used every drug laid before her as research to understand her father, and to proclaim achievement of such a feat, I was left ruminating and confounded.

What would it mean to understand someone else through a substance? How can we, if at all, come to grips with Lexi's concept of research as a practice of deliberately taking on other's affective states? How does allowing oneself to be affected enable understanding, as Lexi claims the drugs did with her father? How do relationships get taken up by emotive states? Take, for instance, as Lexi explains above, that she is simultaneously happy her father didn't get "in trouble" for molesting her, even though she was reprimanded for telling her family about her sexual abuse. The moment she was molested, her "childhood went away," and she became angry. Yet because she loved her dad, she still wanted to understand him and the drugs "that took him away." Her emotional life and her literacies that enable her storytelling are intimately bound up with her attempts to understand her father.

Even through Lexi's seeming contradictory emotional states, she stays resolute throughout the interview, and I think back, wondering how she was able to house such conflicting affections for her father. Lexi's paternal affinity reveals how affects can teach us that being with one another can be learned even when our affective states may exist in contradiction. For instance, Lexi recalls a time she visited her dad in prison. At this point in her life, her drug use primarily involved pot, alcohol, and cocaine. In their prison visit, her dad imparted some wisdom to her: "He told me, 'Don't do cocaine. It's too expensive. Do meth instead.'" Afterward, meth became her drug of choice. It's worth highlighting that Lexi's view of the drug's agency (i.e., "it took") also reveals that drugs have their own agency in her animate literacies. The conglomeration of sexual trauma, drugs, her father, her bisexuality, and so on is all affectively captured in what Lexi calls *research*.

With an understanding that literacy is an exchange of forces, we can see that Lexi is exchanging these relationships into a literacy practice of research during her storytelling. Research literacies has been defined "as the ability to locate, understand, critically evaluate, apply scholarly works—that is, to become discerning and knowledgeable about research."[31] I think Lexi's story offers us a queerer perspective on how research can be an affective literacy practice. Let me explain. Lexi tells me that she wanted to help her dad get clean when she started to sober up herself: "He is still an active user. He is schizophrenic. It's a disease that runs deep in my family. He self-medicates, which is the issue. It's just all he knows. He was just not ready. You can't make someone be ready. It's just something you have to want bad enough. I did want it, but I didn't want it bad enough right away. I still had to experience another drug that took him from me, which is bath salts."

Notice how Lexi understands that willingness is enmeshed with the affect of literacies—her dad must *want* to go. Even she deduces that she "didn't want it bad enough," and desire and feeling are measured in degrees of affect. From this part of her story, I asked her if the rumors of people doing inhumane acts while using bath salts were true. She said she never witnessed or saw anything like that. Instead, she described her experience, or, you could say, she presented her research findings through a lengthy metaphor:

> The way I described meth is a monster with tentacles. It wraps itself around your wrist and says, 'Come follow me,' and so you go. And before you know, it's got you hung; it's got its tentacles wrapped around your throat. And that's what's different [with bath salts]; it immediately grabs you around your throat and says, 'You're coming with me.' It was the first time I felt the addiction. Within a month, I was craving it. It's disgustingly uncomfortable because it hits your central nervous system, and what it does with your central nervous system is that it just shocks it. Your central nervous system doesn't know what's going on, and you can feel it throughout your entire body. When you're on it, your entire body starts to feel *ick*. And I just wanted it; I wanted more.

This lengthy metaphor is important in making sense of Lexi's relationship with drugs and her capacity to make meaning from her experience. The use of metaphor here is not only a literacy affect—Lexi is describing her affective state while she's using meth and bath salts—I'd say that her thick description is akin to field notes and thus a form of empirical research. Considering that empirical research is based on "recorded observations of events," which "often provide a rich understanding of some phenomenon, person, or community," I can't help but see how Lexi's metaphor can be understood as testament to her own literacy practice of researching affective states.[32] She is researching the emotional life of her father, her own use of drugs, and how drugs affect her world overall. This became even clearer when she revealed the next part of her story.

After she explained how bath salts made her feel and her experience of drugs all around, she told me:

> I'm writing a book, actually. I've written poems since I was a teenager, always wanted to publish a novel. I didn't know about what. I know I wanted it to be about me and my life story. I want it to look like a Lifetime movie . . . I've started writing more. I like to date things. I like to see what I'm doing at that moment. I started three years ago just so I can look back and see where I was at the time, so I can see a lot of my [drug] use. When I do drugs, I don't just do them; I look into them before I do them. I do a lot of research before because I want to know what it's going to do to me. I want to know how it's going to feel. I want to know how I'm going to come down off of it. I wanted to do research, and how do you do research if you don't have knowledge of it?

In a small amount of time, Lexi exposes how her poetry, the aspiring process of writing a book, and dreams of writing a novel are intertwined with her experiences. Writing offers her a way into understanding the ways she emotionally lives in the world. The mention of a Lifetime movie stands out because of the sentimentality that accompanies such films. What's more, when she discusses what she writes, she does so through seeing herself. "To look back," "to see," "look into" all suggest that writing and research for Lexi are tangled with her ability to affect the world around her. In fact, it is the world that had prompted her to start "writing more." Then, to keep dates of every time she does a drug also opens up a conversation as to how she is in fact using her emotions to become literate with her affinity of drugs. She says, "I want to know how it's going to feel." Literacy affects move us past mere discernment into emotional and embodied feeling states that connect us to things, and in Lexi's case, the repetition of such research practices led to her addiction.

Thinking of doing drugs as a research literacy practice may not align with our more orthodox understanding of research. I realize, too, that doing drugs may not always be a healthy choice. The argument could be made that Lexi's framing of drug use is justification; I'm not concerned with arguing diagnoses or whether her research practices mask her addiction. Her literacies exist as they are, and I am not attempting to unearth their true motives but rather to explain how they are caught up in and exist as an exchange of forces. Lexi's story is an astute example of how literacy weaves in and out of our emotional lives. She wanted to know how she felt during her research, as she says above. She wanted to make sense of feeling and sensation while she was doing drugs, but I'd argue her feelings were also bolstered by the need to perceive her father and their relationship. Saying she was interested in how she would "come down off" the drug also underscores the literacy affect of doing drugs as research. When you come down from a drug, it metaphorically indicates the high you experience while doing the drugs, pointing to the state of elation and sensation that drugs induce. Lexi wanted to know, to understand, to discern *and* to feel, to emote, to embody what the drugs would do, and by calling it *research*, she shows how unconventional methods can exist in animate literacies when we take into account the affect of literacy.

Elizabeth's Story: Bifurcated Places

Trigger Warning: This Story Contains Strong Religious Condemnation

Elizabeth was born in Kentucky but shortly moved to eastern Tennessee with her mom and dad. She stayed in Tennessee for her entire educational career, going to a high school that "was on the southern parts" of town, "where lower-income people went and where people went who lived out on farms." As an undergraduate, Elizabeth left Appalachia and traveled to central

Tennessee, where it was "flat and had no mountains. It was still a similar culture in some ways" to where she grew up. She told me how she wanted to go to graduate school back East in the mountains and only applied to schools that were "within five or ten miles of home." It was during grad school that Elizabeth would come out as bisexual. She tells me now she has toyed with identifying terms, sometimes referring to herself as *queer*, and is "still exploring they/them pronouns." She also clarified that she does identify as a cisgender woman. For the sake of her story here, I refer to Elizabeth as *she/her* because she is still exploring such queer identities and didn't give me any definitive instructions otherwise.

Elizabeth's story often pivoted from speaking about one place versus another. At multiple instances, she told me stories about her literacy practices in Appalachia and then out of Appalachia. Her story opens a conversation on literacy affects and their ability to form queer affinities with places. Since literacy affects involve our states of being, this section explores how literacy is involved with our being in particular places. For Elizabeth, this takes shape with regard to having a split educational experience in and outside Appalachia, as well as attending two different churches.

When Elizabeth and I talked over the phone during the summer of 2018, she explained to me how she was currently living in rural northern New York. She moved there shortly after graduate school for a job. I asked her what it's like living so far away from home and Appalachia. She said:

> I still live in a place that is very rural. It's still very conservative. It's just in New York state, so it comes with benefits. So, for instance, my partner is trans, and in New York, it is illegal to deny care. Insurance companies have to cover it. So that's been amazing. Even though we are in a conservative area, he can still get the care that he needs. So that's been great. I don't know, it's interesting because the culture isn't that

different. I would've probably experienced a lot of the same things in any rural or conservative setting. I've found that being in Appalachia, there was so much more community. There had to be. We had to be open and proud and out for each other. But up here, it's like we don't need that because we are in a blue state. We still need that; we still need to be a part of a community. It's been interesting. We still haven't been able to tap into that yet here, where it was all very out in the open back in the South. Everywhere that I lived, it was all in Tennessee, Southcentral, there was always an out community.

Elizabeth's story is deeply enmeshed with her relationship to place. Just from this quote alone, particular words like *conservative, rural, place, setting, community, blue state, South* all stand out. And in reference to place, when Elizabeth is discussing a "we" in her story, she is talking about the queer community she and her partner belong to, as she frequently restates throughout our interview. She tells me that "we need" community in Appalachia, whereas in New York, there's an assumption that a queer community "is not needed" due to the liberties associated with New York being a blue and, thus, liberal state. In moments like these, she reveals her relationship to Appalachia as a place where she has found queer community.

I think this association with the queer life Elizabeth experienced in Appalachia being made up of a necessary community has some ties to her love of books and learning. "My mom and my grandmother are both librarians," she told me. "So books and reading was really encouraged in my family." Yet it wasn't only that she was encouraged to read and that she found solace in books; it was the fact that she found herself isolated: "I was a weird kid. . . . I didn't have a lot of friends. Reading was how I spent most of my time. I would read every book in sight. I was drawn to worlds that weren't the world that we live in; fantasy and things like that really took me out of the place that we were in."

Queer Affinities

Place and reading are interconnected for Elizabeth. What stands out in her relationship to books is their ability to transport her away from the Tennessee mountains, which may seem at odds with her lamenting her move away from Appalachia to rural New York after grad school. As if she catches this contradiction immediately, she continues, "But it is really interesting, when I really reflect on it, I connected with characters that were from mountainous regions, from poor regions. It just so happened that that would be part of their character." She came to this conclusion on her own without my asking if her reading related to her Appalachian identity.

She told me, "A lot of the books I read, the protagonist would be a young girl who doesn't have a family anymore, she comes from nowhere, and she conquers whatever it is she has to fight." Reading, for Elizabeth, mediated her experience of self in the mountains. Listening back to and reading the transcript of our interview, it felt at times she was coming to terms with the characters in the books she read. The literacy affect of yearning to belong somewhere else and finding community with fictional characters supports Pritchard's framing of "fictive kin."[33] Fictive kin, or kinship, they write, "refers to characters in books, film, theater, television, music, and other cultural productions that participants described having a connection that felt familial, influential, and lasting."[34] These fictive kin were her community elsewhere, and the only way she could find them was to read, or as she said almost in refrain, "I always read because it allowed me to be in another place." Even though the places she was transported to were often mountainous and poor, as I mentioned in the last paragraph, I'd argue the reason she wanted to leave was due to her lack of belonging to a queer community. I want to be clear: Elizabeth is referring to her Appalachian *childhood* as a heteronormative place to escape; once she came out as an adult, she was able to find her queer community in Appalachia outside of books alone. Elizabeth's affinity with fictional characters queered her relationship with Appalachia before she could find her queer community later in life. As a literacy affect, this last statement is telling. The books evoked an affect. Of course, she is using a metaphor here in saying the books took her to "another place," for she isn't speaking about a literal place in this instance; the fantasy novels allowed her to take on the affective states, however, of another person—in this case, the protagonists she saw as herself.

Elizabeth's affinity for reading not only offered her an exit strategy out of the mountains but also permitted her reentry. After college, on entering grad school, it becomes clear that she was able to find the queer community she often returns to in her story because of her academic work and successes. Elizabeth doesn't reveal specifics as far as what she studies or where she went to school; when I asked her about specific locations or details like her field of work, she told me she'd "prefer not to say." She did tell me, however, that she researches "instances of stigma that people experience and how that relates to mental and physical health disparities," focusing specifically "on the queer community." Elizabeth's research again brings up questions of how we take on affective states of others, regardless if Elizabeth's research is more aligned with academic research compared to Lexi's in the last section. I don't believe the two are that far off when it comes to research as a literacy practice, however, and this is especially true when taking into account that both Lexi and Elizabeth are "researching" how others embodied their lives.

To think of this point in the converse, both Elizabeth and Lexi can be considered researchers. Maybe Ann Berthoff was on to something when she says that in order to understand how "REsearch, like REcognition, is a REflexive act . . . it helps to pronounce 'research' the way southerners do."[35] I'm a Southerner like Elizabeth, and I believe that Berthoff's unintended slight to our syllabic inflection illustrates to what extent place is truly mediated in our languaging. Our literacies have affinities with places; place in turn affects how we read in the world and read the world. I'm not discounting Berthoff's argument—I agree with her that research requires "looking and looking again."[36]

Queer Affinities

However, by using the stereotypes of Southern accentuation, she implicates place into literacy practices and inadvertently shows that how we talk is linked to where we talk, and where we research is integral to how we research.

Pressing this line of thinking further, when literacy practices are affected by place, you could say that place bifurcates the relationships between self and communities; place demarcates how we articulate ourselves in relationship to our communities. To put it another way, where we become literate separates and enables a recognition of the self from the community. What led me to this thinking was a specific moment of Elizabeth's story. Elizabeth explained in our discussion of her religion and spirituality that she had a "bifurcated experience growing up." What she meant is this:

> My mom went to a church, the United Church of Christ, which is super, super liberal. They're very open and accepting. But then, when I was in third or fourth grade, my parents got a divorce. My dad started going to a Baptist church across the town. His mom is Baptist, and even though he was super religious, he was just wanting to connect to a community that he was familiar with. That experience was much more conservative. I remember when I was about twelve or so, we were at the Baptist church, and the pastor said something, "All gays are going to hell." And I told my dad afterwards that I didn't want to go back. I remember that being one of the first instances it became really clear to me that people use religion however they want, for whatever agenda they have for themselves. I grew up really steeped in that religiosity.

Elizabeth's bifurcation occurs at several places. Her parents divorcing separated how she understood her familial unit. This takes shape specifically through the two churches she now went to. Not knowing much about the United Church of Christ

(UCC) myself, I was curious as to what Elizabeth meant when she said it was "super, super liberal."

In 1975, the 10th General Synod of the UCC passed a pronouncement on "Civil Liberties without Discrimination Related to Affectional or Sexual Preference."[37] The pronouncement did not aim "to make an ethical judgment about same-gender relationships" but instead to "clarify the ethical issues involved in human sexuality."[38] Interestingly enough, despite this first instance of declaring support for nonheterosexual church members, the pronouncement argues for government legislation to ensure the ethical treatment of gays and lesbians: "Further, the Tenth General Synod declares its support for the enactment of legislation at the federal, state and local levels of government that would guarantee the liberties of all persons without discrimination related to affectional or sexual preference."[39] Even within the dogma of the church, literacy shapes how queerness is treated by proxy of places. The UCC relies on laws of the land, so to speak, to mediate its collective views on the treatment of LGBTQ+ folx.

The UCC would go on to fully own its call "for an end to rhetoric that fuels hostility, misunderstanding, fear and hatred expressed toward gay, lesbian, bisexual and transgender persons."[40] And it's endearing to know that the UCC was the first church to openly ordain a gay pastor in 1972. I argue that the literacy acts of the UCC—the passing of the pronouncements, the advocating for changes to the state legislation, even having an internal legislative order, the Synod in the church—mediates how Elizabeth's religion is practiced in particular places, even if only, in her experience, she is affected by this by her going across town to another church.

Moreover, in terms of literacy affects, the bifurcated experience of attending two different churches for Elizabeth extends beyond the literacy practices of the church at large. The preacher in the Baptist church declaring that "all gays are going to hell" affected twelve-year-old Elizabeth as much as, I believe, the Elizabeth who was retelling these stories. Even the statement that queers are "going to hell" implies that literacies move us and affect how we are oriented to particular places. Hell as a destination is literal, I think, for evangelical Christians. This is true if you take a trip and drive on most interstates in the Midwest or South. You're bound to end up passing a "Hell Is Real" billboard. Elizabeth doesn't bring up hell anywhere but this instance of quoting the pastor, but in her retelling, she invokes the historic affect of hate that's withstanding in such religious discourse.

Eventually, Elizabeth found her community of queers in Appalachia. She told me she realized "family is so much bigger" once she found her partner and her community during graduate school. If literacy affects expose that, through our stories, our affinities with places are affected by literacy practices, then Elizabeth's view of family was certainly mediated by her literacies of place. She told me how using the internet to stay connected to her chosen family back in Appalachia is important and explained that she oftentimes searches Instagram for #OurMountainsToo, a hashtag for queers to claim their place in the mountains where they live. She also tells me of the "queersgivings" they still have when she visits. Yet what I'll keep with me from having talked with Elizabeth, the part of her story that affected me the most, is this: "We can make the places we need." She's right, I think. Queers and their literacy practices, even in the mountains—which are our mountains too—can create places worth living in and being with.

Macy's Story: Sexual Literacy and Resisting Bi-Erasure

Trigger Warning: This Story Contains
Rape and Sexual Assault

Macy grew up in southern Ohio, and as she put it, "Kentucky was in my backyard." She was twenty-two at the time of our interview and still finishing college in Ohio. Macy's story is fascinating, for her narrative complicates sexual literacy practices as being bound up and enmeshed with literacy affects. She came out in college, she told me, in 2017, just a year prior to our conversation. Macy explained that as a kid, she didn't have access to the vocabulary to understand queer issues: "My computer usage was restricted at home growing up. I had no resources. I couldn't look up 'gay' on the computer or 'LGBTQ+' resources. I didn't even know what LGBTQ+ meant." I asked her, "Do you think your queerness is connected to having access to the knowledge and the language because you didn't have any of the connections at home as you did at college?" Her answer was:

> This is funny. I'm remember something from sixth grade. There was this one book in my middle school library that was about queerness. It was really weird. It was a very weird book, and I have no idea what the title was, but it argued that being gay is a religion. And people should have the same rights to get married. I was very confused, so I rolled with it. It was the only thing I knew, but I knew intuitively that LGBTQ+ people should have the [same] rights as everyone else did. But I didn't know anything [about queerness], so I think that that [i.e., the gay religion argument] was a thing for three years.

Later in high school, she told me, she found out what gay was because there was a gay pediatrician in town whom some parents wouldn't take their kids to because "they called him a faggot." It wasn't till she "was an orientation leader at college" that she "would stay quiet and listen to LGBT stuff when it came up in training."

After she accessed queer sexual literacy as an orientational leader in college, she told me that she identifies as pan. However, she typically tells everyone she is bisexual because of the labor required to explain pansexuality. In her own words:

> I usually tell people that I'm bisexual, but I identify as pan. The reason I choose when asked or in [particular]

spaces is because a lot of people don't know what it means to be pan. Bisexual, a lot of people already knows what that means. Usually where I'm from and the people who I grew up with, there are already so many educational roles I have to take on for them. And explaining what pan is on top of all that is just too much. I identify with bi-erasure. I don't think bi-erasure is OK, but I've experienced it all my life. And saying that I'm bisexual ties in more closely with my experiences.

The prefix *pan-* comes from the Greek for *all*. Thus, pansexuals are attracted to all valences of gender, not merely limited to male or female gender expressions. I find it striking that there are connections between the Arcadian god Pan, the half-goat, horned deity who preferred the limitless countryside to walled-up city limits, and pansexuality, which is not bound by culture's limits for desiring gender. Also, it's compelling how the word *panic* comes directly from the associations of Pan the god since he threatened civilization's rules, much like how Macy's pansexuality may cause those around her to panic if they found out she wasn't attracted to only two genders (or even revealed that there are more than two genders, for that matter).

Macy's statement stands out because she makes clear that being literate can regularly come with expanding one's energy in order to affect others' literacies. In her taking on "many educational roles" for the people in her hometown is an implicit indication that she is literate in ways they aren't: the "role" to educate she has to step into is the role of a literacy sponsor, which is to say that Macy acts to make others more literate in what they know, bringing home from college the knowledge she has garnered. The labor that is spent for Macy comes at a higher cost, however, when you consider that it isn't just what she knows that makes her a literacy sponsor but because her literacy is tangled with her queer identity. When Macy chooses where and under which conditions to disclose she is pansexual, she is discussing the affective labor of being a sexual literacy sponsor.

When Macy says she identifies with bi-erasure, she is referring to the phenomena of being made to feel as though one's bisexuality is frivolous or not legitimate. When bisexuality is dismissed as inauthentic, sheer indecisiveness, or even considered not to be real, it's erasing bisexuality from the queer spectrum. Early queer theorists, like Lee Edelman and Eve Sedgwick, have been critiqued for ignoring bisexuality in theoretical terms of queerness.[41] As of late, bisexuality has resurfaced in cultural studies in a number of ways, for instance, with regard to intersectionality along gendered and racial lines or examining legislative discourse for acknowledgment of bisexuality.[42] The *Journal of Bisexuality* was established in 2000 in response to these issues and to make more visible the B in LGBTQ+ studies.

The feeling of having an illegible sexuality affected by bi-erasure was more than a mere aspect of Macy's labor endured through naming her desire; it affected her embodied life in her relationships. Macy continues to explain how coming out as bisexual has led her to experience violent trauma:

> I didn't come out in any way until I was in college. I chose to tell [the man she was in a relationship with] because I was coming to terms with my sexuality, and I wanted to tell someone that would support me. A lot of people in my [home] area believed that being gay is a sin. So I shared it with him, and then over the next two to three months of our relationship, he became very violent. Emotionally, physically, verbally. He said that I told him because I want to be with women. That I'm not sexually satisfied by him.

Macy's use of "coming to terms" may be read here as more literal even though it's a figurative phrase since she was developing a terminology for her desire; she was coming to the words that named her identity. The affect people back home had on Macy is worth recognizing, too, when they equate gayness with sinfulness. Like Justin and Elizabeth, Macy wasn't able to come out until she was in college, outside of Appalachia. Macy's particular instance of coming out, though, is one that resonates and *feels* less about having to be outside of Appalachia and more about feeling secure enough come out. Although Macy thought her boyfriend would be supportive, he ultimately turned violent because he thought she couldn't simply be bisexual because bisexuality was incompatible with his sexual literacy; for him, it was an excuse to be gay, or it was an explanation of *his* inability to give her pleasure. In short, and in Macy's own words, her bisexuality "threatened his masculinity."

Not only is the boyfriend threatened in this case; so is heteronormativity and its reliance on binary logics. Macy's bisexuality and her development of bisexuality in her sexual literacy operate from a "both/and" topoi rather than the "either/or" logics that underscore bi-erasure. Through this thinking, arguably the volatility of bisexuality may be the most disruptive in the queer spectrum of sexualities in terms of disrupting animacy hierarchies altogether. That is to say, bisexuality does not fit into enthymematic sense-making but bursts open such syllogisms even within gay and lesbian frameworks. For example, you are either gay *or* straight; if you are x (e.g., a man or woman), and you desire y (e.g., same-sex partners or opposite partners), then you are z (e.g., gay or straight). Macy used the word *threat* in reference to her boyfriend, but because they were in a "straight" relationship before her coming out, the threat is also connected to preconditioned affective state of comfort that supposedly accompanies heteronormative relationships. Recall that queer affects fail to reproduce the scripts of heterosexuality, with its "function as a form of public comfort by allowing bodies to extend into space that have already taken their shape"[43] Macy's body by way of her desire broke the comfortable space in their relationship, and unfortunately her body became the site of her boyfriend's abuse.

She details the extent of the violence: "It was interesting because I am a very monogamous person. I didn't have any interests in anyone but him. So that really hurt me because at first I thought these are valid questions, valid concerns. Then all of a sudden it transformed to another level. He made me take pregnancy tests every day, even when I was on my period, because he was convinced that because [if] I was bi, [then] I was so sexual and cheating on him."

Eventually, after Macy told her mom of her boyfriend's irrational and dangerous behavior, her mom all but forced her to break up with him while letting her do it at her mom's house as a precaution. Macy explains that "at this point, it hadn't been too incredibly physically violent." She says that she only had a few bruises on her arms where "he grabbed" her "too hard, but it wasn't alarming yet." Two months later, the boyfriend showed up to her apartment while her roommate was out of town. Macy told me that he "found out because he saw my roommate was [out of town] on Snapchat, so he chose to drive up" to her college town and to her apartment. "I knew his grandma had died and he was sad, so I let him in. Then he physically and sexually assaulted me," she said. Continuing to narrate this moment, Macy explained, "During that assault, he came over when he had a cold sore, and part of that assault was infecting me with herpes. He told me he wanted to do that because then I would never be able to have sex with women, because his idea of sex with women was exclusively oral sex, and no girl would want to go down on me if I had herpes."

There are plenty of emotionally laden issues at play here. For instance, when Macy begins to recall how hurt she felt that the legitimacy of their monogamous relationship was questioned exposes how her relationship was endured because of pain. That is, Macy withstood the abuse because of her own emotional state in order to show that she was, in fact, monogamous.

The idea of Macy's boyfriend forcing her to take pregnancy tests is disturbing, yet it demonstrates the heteropatriarchy's precarious state of fragility. Thinking about fragility on its own as an affect, outside of the context of Macy's story, for a moment may help illuminate why Macy was willing to endure such violent abuse. To be fragile, to require careful handling, to be delicate as an affective state places an immense amount of responsibility on the bodies around the fragile body. You treat the expensive china with a sensitive touch. Don't drop the fragile fluorescent light bulb because, if it shatters, the mercurial dust may contaminate your bloodstream. Fragile label warnings provide an interesting visual cue as to how bodies that are fragile are meant to be treated:

Credit: SeekPNG

Notice that the hands around the box—the fragile body here—gesture toward the embodied labor of treating a fragile body with care; it is the responsibility of the hands, and of the body to which the hands belong, to take care, to exert labor, to be mindful of the affective state of the body it must touch and act on. The directional arrows of the second icon are particularly revealing. Fragile actors must be kept in particular lines of orientation. The image here insists that we keep the fragile body *upright* as to protect its precarity. Conceiving of *up* in an animacies framework hierarchizes the agency of fragile bodies to be kept only in one position; the bodies interacting with the fragile ones must accommodate around their straight, *right*, "correct" position. The image of the cracked glass suggests the true nature of fragility is the assumption of the body's broken state, as to say that this object contains within it an already brokenness that we must avoid at all costs. Those costs come from protecting the fragility, which I believe is meant to be the intended meaning of the umbrella. Shield. Protect. Deflect. The fragile body is one that is already broken unless thwarted through the labor of other bodies.

Macy's boyfriend takes on the animacy of a fragile body because her bisexuality refuses to uphold their relationship in the ways her sexuality did before. The labor of reaffirming his straightness was no longer about her keeping him and their heterosexual relationship comfortable. In fact, Macy's sexuality shows that there are other lines of orientation that stretch out in multiple directions. She no longer has to keep fragile masculinity in the upright position; she can take a more crooked path. Her boyfriend, by questioning his ability to give her pleasure, shows the crack in the veneer of masculinity like the cracked glass of the fragile warning label. Turning her coming out into an issue about himself and his capability to produce pleasure inculcates his already state of brokenness—in his self-view, he was already inadequate. When Macy folds up her umbrella, she leaves him exposed to his own insecurities.

However, Macy doesn't immediately reach the point of leaving him or realizing this; it took her time and happened only after he sexually assaulted her. Recall that Macy initially understood her boyfriend's reaction as "valid questions, valid concerns." She endured his fragility because her sexuality up until this moment fit into systemic compulsory heterosexuality that gives more agency to men; the patriarchy is as much about affective, ontological hierarchies as it is about gender. This becomes readily apparent through the coercive pregnancy tests. Think of the pregnancy test as an apparatus in the new materialist sense, where "apparatuses are specific material reconfigurings of the world that do not merely emerge in time but iteratively reconfigure space-time-matter as part of the ongoing dynamism of."[44] Through the forced pregnancy tests, Macy's boyfriend iteratively renders his own heterosexual literacy: anything outside the logics of compulsory heterosexuality would indicate Macy was cheating on him. In other words, the romantic relationship between Macy and her boyfriend is measured by her embodiment, her capacity to now be "so sexual" by her bi-ness that he needs to reconfigure the fragile structures that his own sexual literacy practices were built on—the tests were an apparatus to allow this to occur.

Macy stayed for three years in a relationship with her abusive boyfriend because, as she says, "she was coming to terms" with or was in the process of becoming sexually literate and was not yet able to make meaning of her boyfriend's behavior. She was only able to break the relationship once she told stories of her experiences to others. Her mom, as she said, "basically made me break up with him." Since sexual literacy "engages the stories we tell about sex and sexuality to probe them for controlling values and for ways to resist, when necessary, constraining norms," I believe that Macy was only able to resist the harm that affected her from her boyfriend and the toxic relationship when she was able to express her own story and make it comprehensible in her relationship with her mom.[45] This issue becomes more complex considering that the boyfriend, after the breakup, intended to infect her with herpes so she couldn't have sex with women (his perception being that same-sex lesbian sex is strictly oral).

The assault Macy experiences underpins literacy affects' investment in literacy moving in a flow of sorts. Don't mistake my saying that literacy was present for literacy taking on some agency in the assault. Instead, literacy was not merely an inert force in the series of events that led up to Macy's attack. As I've pointed out already, she had developed sexual literacy of coming out, of challenging the stories of sexuality she had been told in order to play a role (as did the ex's interaction with social media such as Snapchat). Animate literacies are ever moving in matrices of actors, places, sexualities, desires, and so forth. Paying attention to literacy affects reveals this interconnectedness and how literacy is ever passed back and forth. Think of Macy's statement that she "knew his grandma had died and he was sad," so she "let him in." The literacy affect of sympathizing is an extension of the threatened-ness the ex-boyfriend felt even months after the literacy event of Macy's coming out.

Macy wasn't infected. She didn't press charges. She said she didn't involve the law because she "didn't want her life showcased" publicly—and reasonably so when keeping in mind that it was the bi-erasure that set off the series of events initially; it is understandable that she would not want to risk feeling as though her sexuality was at fault or to blame again in reporting it to the police. In many ways, Macy's story echoes Lexi's from a few pages back. Lexi felt like her bi-ness wasn't taken seriously. Macy and Lexi both shared with me the pressures of having systemic legislative forces affect their own sexual literacy. Lexi's husband was threatened, as was Macy's boyfriend. Two women owning their sexual literacy narrative, owning their story and bisexuality, were eclipsed by fragile masculinity. Literacy isn't to blame; literacy isn't without blame. Literacy and its affects linger in our sexual affinities, moving and shifting, a constant reconfiguration of affiliations.

Lara's Story: The Conquest of the Condom

This last story belongs to Lara. When Lara and I spoke over the phone in June 2018, Lara was attending an Appalachian private liberal arts college in Kentucky. She came to Kentucky at fifteen years old, moving with her mom from New Mexico when her distant relatives kicked them out. She goes home during breaks and during the summer when she isn't in college. She told me, "I'm bisexual," and "I consider myself cisgender female, but I've kinda been going through this time where I'm more gender fluid, genderqueer. As of now, I'm still [identifying] as cisgender." She grew up thinking that "you were either gay or straight"; she said she "didn't know that you could like both." Growing up, she enjoyed school: "Did well, very well, in school. Always on the honor roll. I think I made three Cs my entire high school career. I cried about it because I made a 79." She puts it simply: "I loved it. I loved learning." The emotional connection to learning, education, and literacy became abundantly clear as I listened to Lara.

I end this chapter with Lara's story because, in its own way, it strings together the previous three stories. Her story in particular links together how literacy affects move us, flow through our communities and our sexuality, foster a sense of place. Lara told me a number of times that she is passionate about school. She even referred to herself as "a doer," being very active on campus. She explained how she initiated a group on campus in 2017: "This last year, I started a club, Generation Action, working with Planned Parenthood. Our goal for campus is to get out there and teach our peers sexual reproductive health care, teaching them sex-care education. We do events on campus, host panels; we've done all sorts of different things this year. I found that passion, that sexual health education."

I asked her what brought her to that passion, and she said:

> It's a very funny story. On Facebook during my sophomore year, scrolling through Facebook and saw this ad that said *free condoms*. "Do you want free condoms?" Who the hell wouldn't want free condoms? I clicked on it, and it was an application. I thought it was going to be something like a free sample of Lifestyles [a brand of condoms], but it was an application for the Great American Condom Campaign [ACC]. It's a campaign for the organization Advocates for Youth that Trojan [the condom company] has. They will send you five hundred free condoms to hand out to the student body. You hand out condoms and educate how to use condoms properly. You hand out information about consent. [Trojan] has a whole culture of consent campaign that goes along with the ACC.

She "kept learning and learning and learning" on her own, through classes, on the internet, and from the ACC, and, as she puts it, she "realized, holy shit!"—sexual education in America "needs to be fixed." She was, like Lexi and Elizabeth, a researcher. Moreover, like Macy, she began to take on the role of a sexual literacy sponsor but not because of her sexuality or her personal relationships but because her digital literacies led her to condoms. Lots and lots of condoms.

Because the ACC had an incentive program built into it—the more you accomplished in spreading sexual health knowledge, the more merchandise you received—Lara began to use her campus as a place to "hand out condoms and educate how to use condoms properly," as I quote above. I like to think she is spreading the good word of the condom. She told me this led to "getting the attention of our vice president of Student Affairs. He called me into his office," she explained, because "it got to the point where we needed to get all these condoms in the dorms." Lara talked to all the collegium, who were "all gung-ho, *let's go for it.*" So she talked to her Student Government Association president, who permitted her to place condoms in the dorms. Once their condoms found their way into the dormitories, she was contacted by the vice president for Student Life, the boss of the collegium staff. He had no idea about the condoms supplied now campus-wide. Explaining that Lara wasn't in any trouble, he just wanted to know who gave her permission to put condoms in the student housing. He told her, "'I am really interested in this, and I have been thinking about doing something like this for a while. But we can't put condoms out without having education about them,' he said. He explained that he wanted to form a Health Care Education Committee that I would have an active role in developing."

The committee was formed in spring 2017, which started the "slowest process ever" in developing policy. She said she is someone who "wants to get in there and do things and not spend five meetings discussing the wording of our mission." I think this last statement demonstrates through a framework of animate literacies that we can see how traditional models of literacies may not always function to explain the complete view of what literacy is or what it can do. We could focus on the writing itself. What words were used. Who and why did they halt the process. How the policy was implemented. Animate literacies broaden our focus here to include all actors and the affects they had.

In Lara's view, literacy practices of writing policy were actually getting in the way of affecting the world around her. "It's frustrating being on that committee," she told me, "because we haven't done anything." When Lara says they haven't done anything, she is pointing to the moment where language can sometimes hinder action. Even though policy writing is still doing something, in Lara's view, the policy doesn't affect real life until it functions outside of the bickering over word choice and semantics. She told me that "the next year's team will be able to do a lot more" and "move forward" because the "clerical work is out of the way." In this way, traditional literacy comes to stifle the queer routes of animate literacies and their literacy affects. Reading and writing can clash with animate literacies, and the friction it causes still *does something in the world.*

Perhaps the most brilliant part of Lara's story, in my opinion, is her and her committee's goal to make available free menstruation products on campus. The committee has "gone out and bought pads and some tampons but mostly pads because it's easier to provide" considering the cost. Because the committee is working with limited funds, they have chosen "really populated places on campus" to provide the sanitary products because they can't "afford to put them in the dorms yet." She explained, "We've made it very clear that they [i.e., the pads and tampons] are going in both the male and female restroom." Their aim? Inclusivity. The way Lara put it is, "It's a conversation starter. *Why are you putting pads in the boys' bathroom?* Well, you don't know if a female-to-male trans person is going to go in there and might need a tampon."

Here's how it all comes together: As literacy sponsors, both Lara *and* the hordes of condoms *and* the consent pamphlets *and* the individuals in the college's government *and* the tampons *and* the pads *and* bathrooms *and, and, and*: all of these actors are flowing into and out of literacies the entire time. Literacy is exchanging its forces on Facebook for Lara. The exchange took place in her vice president's office. The exchange became blocked during the five quarrelsome meetings. The exchanges are caught up in a torrent of literacies that enable Lara to feel frustrated, to queer men's bathrooms by including menstrual hygiene products, to feel passionate about sexual health, *to effect change and be with* one another on Lara's college campus.

Animate literacies revel in the jamboree of actors and their affective potential for world-makings. Animate literacies also realize that the world is wrought and teeming with pain, trauma, and hatred and make room for literacy studies to bring those emotions, feelings, affects into our disciplinary home, making room at the table. Animate literacies are about finding the ontological aspects of literacy that fall to the side when we only focus on *who* can read and *what* they are reading or who can write and what they are writing. I say this fully embracing my queer and scholarly selves: animate literacies see literacy as an orgy of reading/writing/knowing/doing/being together in a world so dense with meaning that we will never be able to find the truth behind it all—we best learn how to get along with one another in more creative, queerer ways instead. The forces that were at play in Lara's story, as it is in all the stories in this entire project, reflect back through storytelling the potential to connect, to be with each. Yes, undoubtedly, the force of literacy can be exchanged as an ability to read and write; literacy as an exchange of forces, however, isn't only an ability possessed—the energetic flow of forces that make animate literacies possible is about finding more affiliations that make living life full of queer possibilities.

5

Carrying Mountains to the Sea

The Cape Cod Canal was brought to life in seven years. Its first shovel of earth was removed in 1909 and the last bit of shell rock swept out of the way by engineering ingenuity in 1914. A manmade feat, the canal flows in both directions: a tidal force pulls both north toward the Bostonian coastline and southward into the dredges of Buzzard Bay daily, changing every six hours. For a Kentuckian who didn't see the ocean till he was twenty-one, it's difficult still, even as I write this final chapter, to think that I can look out my classroom windows and see its ebb and flow while students huddle about.

Where I teach now is a maritime institution—the ocean, arguably, animates the ins and outs of the entire school. Massachusetts Maritime Academy (MMA) is one of six special maritime mission universities in the United States. As one would reckon, they all are coastal and wrap around the nation, from Maine and Massachusetts to New York and then Texas, California, and even on the shoreline of the Great Lakes in Michigan. They aren't located in mountainous areas. The land here is something else. Often flat and sandy, my commute to the Cape takes me past New England trees that are colored out of a Hallmark movie: cranberry bogs tinged crimson in the fall and then by oceanic inlets and saltwater marshes year round, which I'm still not accustomed to. It isn't unusual for my mind to try and overlay the hills of Kentucky, folded neatly away in memory, with the views that I take in on the regular. The landscape is different here; I feel different in this environment.

I'm concluding *Reading, Writing, and Queer Survival* in a different manner as well. I'd like to end with what it means to be an Appalachian expat living, teaching, and writing in New England. Questions that frequent my mind: How do my students see and hear me differently? How does a queer Appalachian perspective contribute to a Northern university? Does my Appalachian-ness linger? How do reading and writing keep it alive? What's more, the ways we queers navigate the world are largely guided by the literacies we learned belonging to Appalachia. In a number of ways, exposing the often conflicting narratives of queerness—the queer mythos that to be happy is to leave your rural home and be an urbanite—and of Appalachian identity—to be Appalachian is to belong to the region—permits us a space to discuss how literacy connects us to places even when we are hundreds or thousands of miles away. This is critical to keep in mind for those of us who study literacy but perhaps in other ways more important for us Appalachians who couldn't stay, and we had to bring both our queerness and our Appalachian selves across the country. Justin, Lexi, Elizabeth, Macy, and Lara taught me over the years that belonging is movable. *Reading, Writing, and Queer Survival* has taught me to be with my literacies in new ways—a theory of animate literacies as us, as researchers who consider our own literacies as animated, flowing through our worlds as educators.

What follows hopefully is how I see animate literacies come alive outside of the research in the previous pages. This chapter is where I practice what I preach, as my kin would say. My academic friends may call it a chapter on curricular praxis. Its aim, though, is to show how the principles of animate literacies inform my teaching. It displays my own literacy as a queer Appalachian who left Appalachia, invoking the principles of *Reading, Writing, and Queer Survival* throughout the remaining pages. By weaving together story, queerness, place, and pedagogy, I hope other Appalachian expats can think with me about how they carry their multiple Appalachian identities with them into the classroom. I spend time detailing my embodiment and how it informs, en/discourages, propels me to rethink how I teach and analyze a class I designed based on the entire experience, Appalachian Cultures. In other words, much as my participants in the previous chapters learned to survive in ways outside the norm, this conclusion details my own survival miles away from my once home.

Finding Appalachia on Cape Cod

The first semester I taught here, there were many moments when Appalachia fell out of my mouth as if it were bits of coal. Cadets—we're a regimental institution, modeled off a mix of navy and Coast Guard, and our students are referred to as they would be in a military setting—would peer up at me. *What do you mean, Dr. C?* Or, in confusion, I'd respond to a question with a question, *What's a bubbler?* A cadet points to the hallway and asks me what I'd call a water fountain down South. Hell, I can't even swim well enough to tread water, and the cadets regularly take classes on the TS *Kennedy*, a ship that stretches the length of our campus.[1] The *Kennedy* is a federally endowed vessel, routinely making trips up and down the Eastern coast, usually porting in the Mexican Gulf or Caribbean, where students can do nonprofit work for local communities during off-semester winter and summer terms. Understand, my feet are familiar with the foothills and knobs of Kentucky. They sloshed through creek water, are familiar to straw in hayfields, with my toes sinking into limestone-rich soil. Now they find themselves buried in Atlantic sand.

I've discovered that my feet can step into places, keeping upright a queer Kentucky body, with little to no threat of a hate crime. One of their favorite places to pursue is Provincetown, a queer utopian experiment. It took me a while to accept that queers can go about their lives with more ease here than down in my Southern home. Once, a friend walked into a gas station on a beach day wearing a black mesh poncho sans shirt. His nails freshly painted, colored to match his swimming briefs. All without a second thought. My heart went into a flurry. *Hold on*, I worried. *Won't they run us out? They ain't gonna sell us nothing!* He found my paltry apprehension amusing. We continued to Boy Beach with no qualm. Northern queerness ain't always like Appalachian queerness. My body is visibly queer on campus but not in the way that is expected. I'd say it is more queer akin to the way my accent is queer—there's a drawl in my mouth, a smile on my face that reminds me of how a server down home may say, *How ya doing, darlin? Are y'all ready to order?* But in a classroom: *How y'all doing? We ready to git started?* Northern sensibilities aren't necessarily less kind, but smiling at strangers can be an alien nicety in public. I once was told, *Caleb, you don't have to say hi to everyone you pass on the street.* It's that kind of queer, a queerness where I'm trying to meld American regions, making them meet in some way that defies geography. My students get that. In fact, I've made my career here around the seeming incompatibility of an Appalachian queer teaching in a maritime educational ecosystem.

I realized in a short time that being a humanities professor is more freeing than entering into a program where I'm siloed into only the writing and rhetoric curriculum, say, in an English department one would expect to belong to after PhD literacy graduate work. As humanity faculty, we're expected to shoulder both introductory literature and writing courses while given the opportunity to explore other ways to express our research in our class design elsewhere in our electives. Our institution is a STEM university; we only award baccalaureates of science. We have seven majors, two of which are credentialed with administering licenses, or a Standards of Training, Certification, and Watchkeeping, STCW for short, enabling cadets to work at sea immediately out of college. I've helped cadets in my Technical and Business Writing courses go on to be marine merchants, work in the shipping industry or the FBI, while some go on to run fishing businesses or be first responders. The humanities courses are a required component of the general education on campus, with social sciences alongside science and mathematics making up the other two departmental branches. There are days that I miss teaching in an English department geared toward not only fulfilling the requirements of college writing and English majors but also that has an integrated graduate program. There are perks, however, in belonging to what's been described to me as a "supporting department." Without the pressure of recruiting students to join the major, you find that you can embrace a sense of openness to imagine an exploratory curriculum. More tailored to my own research, I can teach without the need to find the English majors waiting dormant in composition classrooms.

Our department is small. I was one of seven when I joined and realized my colleagues often taught special topic courses that would pass through faculty governance, eventually becoming part of the standard course catalog. Usually these special topic and upper-level courses are taken by soon-to-be graduates who need a humanities elective on the precipice of entering into the job market. In my third year on my tenure track, I decided that after studying and publishing at the intersection of Appalachia, rhetoric, new materialist, and queer studies, it was about time I'd design a course around Appalachia in spring 2022. This class, though, had an extra element of personal connection—it was about my home, my heritage, the land that made me a scholar. Potentially teaching a course so close to my worldview could result in failed expectations. Was I setting myself up for disappointment? It was more than mere teaching; it was meaningful in ways that I hadn't experienced as an instructor. The course was ambitious. Faced with the standard issue of how to cover all (not realistic) the material I wanted to in the class, I at least narrowed it down to the following description: "Often called America's other, Appalachia is an American geographic region, culture, and heritage that much of the time is reduced to stereotypes of white rednecks, hillbillies, and the uneducated poor. This course challenges those narratives, expanding on the history of Appalachia to garner a deeper understanding of a place in the US that has contributed to the shaping of our nation and society. Students will spend time with the history, cultural practices, literature, art, folxways, and other ways of living in the mountains to gain more nuanced knowledge of what it means to be Appalachian."

Another shift I had to grapple with was what it meant for a scholar who studies literacy to not name literacy/ies in the title or anywhere in the course objectives. Using "Culture" in the title was selfishly a marketing ploy, I'll admit. We need students to run classes, and at the time, I thought mentioning reading and writing wouldn't be an appropriate means of drawing students to a general education requirement. I had to make it appealing, balance the workload of seniors anticipating running an engine on a ship and needing licensure; they weren't there because they were English majors. But looking back, especially through the lens of what I've been writing on in *Reading, Writing, and Queer Survival*, culture is the conduit through which literacies can flow.

Culture and literacy are a quilt, woven together with thread of similar colors. Culture funnels material actors and affective realities of its participants' literacies. Appalachian culture is also a matter of Appalachian literacies. My objectives in teaching were to help students grapple with the complex definitions of Appalachia; gain an understanding of Appalachian history, how American history shapes the idea of Appalachia, and how Appalachian culture can resist such framings; challenge stereotypes and analyze the treatment of Appalachia in social sciences, media, literature, and the arts; think about the complexities of Appalachian identity, with its many overlaps and intersections of gender, sexuality, race, social class, and ability; appreciate the value of Appalachian culture within American contexts. I was attempting to animate Appalachia.

Scaffolding Appalachia

MMA is a teaching institution, unionized along with nine other teaching universities across the Commonwealth. With teaching as the emphasis and not a heavy lift of research required of faculty, our course load is a staggering 4:4. So in choosing materials for scaffolding your classes, you must be strategic to protect your own time and balance your approach in order to make sure students are learning in your classrooms. One method I found to survive the high demands of four courses is to cross-pollinate materials. I had recently written a chapter on Carter Sickels's *The Prettiest Star*, a queer Appalachian novel, and now I'd be teaching it. What better opportunity to engage with queer literacies than in a course on Appalachia? *The Prettiest Star* made it on the syllabus. Later, Sickles would deliver a reading and Q&A for the cadets. But more on the guests to come.

Affordable materials for students are another collective goal for public universities in Massachusetts. Open educational resources, or OERs, are freely sourced materials that instructors can utilize in lieu of high-priced textbooks. Keeping costs under fifty dollars is one of the goals for OER education. I kept this in mind as I chose the other readings in the class. Elizabeth Catte's *What You Are Getting Wrong about Appalachia* was a formative text in my book here, and I'd argue is an excellent primer for the entire field and discipline of Appalachian studies. If I added it to the reading list, the total costs for the class were under the dollar threshold. I decided that I'd supply the rest of the readings as library-sourced PDF articles. It's important that I frame the costs because it speaks to access in Appalachia. I think back to what I experienced as a college student, oftentimes having to eat out of dumpsters and trash cans because I couldn't afford food when I was a first-year undergrad, let alone the overpriced textbooks. The cost of teaching materials is an Appalachian issue like the educational goals here in the progressive state of Massachusetts. Even in the designing of my classes, I'm *still* affected by where I came from. Did I make this a topic of conversation with the students in my class? No. But it's important to bring up, especially in conversation with a radical text such as Catte's, wherein she offers a scathing polemic against neoliberalism in Appalachia. Appalachian sensibilities are never too far out of reach.

Speaking of progressive critique, I should also discuss the hesitancy I experienced in considering Catte for my syllabus, especially if places matter for living literacies. MMA is in Bourne, Massachusetts. While the majority of the state is colored deeply blue and is especially thought of as a liberal hub in the collective mind's eye of Southern states, Bourne could be considered a translucent red. Bourne might easily be the distant cousin, twice removed from Harlan County, Kentucky. Forty-nine percent of its residents voted for Trump in 2016. Driving along the residential streets into campus, even into the 2020 election, MAGA propaganda peppered the Cape Cod–style homes, RVs, work trucks, and flag poles. The irony still isn't lost on me coming from Kentucky, having lived in Ohio and West Virginia: this didn't feel like Trump country down below the Mason-Dixon. I recognize, much as Catte does, that politics aren't reduced to simple hues. Much as Appalachia isn't monolithically right leaning, Massachusetts isn't unified behind liberal policy in toto.

I don't think it is coincidental that MMA is in a red county, either. Much of our student demographic comes from "blue-collar" families. It isn't unusual that students in my class write about how they grew up on the ocean with their family's fishing business or how they like to work with their hands on engines. Or their parents are alumni, and it's a matter of tradition. Here's another interesting factoid: MMA didn't accept women until 1977. Most of our students are still male and unsurprisingly white. There have been significant changes with the new incoming academic administration that joined in 2019, developing task forces to bring in a more diverse student body and protect diverse faculty. The Office of Intercultural Engagement was developed in the same year as well, with its inclusive outreach efforts. But there is still a lingering aura on campus that conceals conservative politics. It takes a certain grit to be a faculty member here. Faculty of color and women faculty have left because they were met with resistance on campus. It's changing, but I sense it still, especially as a queer person. I think I'm able to dig my feet in for the long haul because I am white, I am cisgender, and I can leverage those identities in my classroom for the sake of supporting and advocating on behalf of the cadets who are underrepresented. Maybe it's easier to discuss race-sex-gender-complex identities when I look like many of the bodies in the classroom. But here's the kicker: I think I'm able to weather some of the pushback because I'm Appalachian. If I survived in a mountain region—which can be hostile toward queerness—as a queer, surely I can do it here in a state that insulates my more progressive thinking. To that end, what would my students think when they read a book that openly rejected Appalachia as Trump country? How would they react to a scathing reproach to reducing Appalachia to a conservative political juggernaut? I'd soonly see.

A major objective that had to be met was the teaching of basic facts and information about Appalachia. It was my goal to challenge myself as an instructor to think about Appalachia in all its plurality. The first question I would pose to the students was *How many Appalachias are there?* In this multifaceted, open-ended inquiry, I framed four central pathways to possible answers: (1) Appalachias exist geographically, (2) via government, (3) by cultural definitions, and (4) regionally within the context of the United States. We watched a documentary on the formation of the mountain range itself. We'd also cover at length how the government sought to frame the region using the ARC, state-level involvement, and federal investment in the war against poverty. These four areas would contextualize the rest of the semester.

I wanted student work in the class to be structured around research with an eye to positionality. The students would learn that outsiders have always inserted themselves into the region, and it was important to be sensitive to this fact as students who were taking the class in the Northeast. The first project was a rolling, ongoing assignment that was completed independently outside of class. Each student was assigned either a notable Appalachian or a specific place in Appalachia, and they would be responsible for teaching the class about their topic through a presentation and developing a quick reference guide. There were also group projects that asked students to understand how socioeconomic and ecological issues manifested in several ways, and their research would require them to think broadly about their topic, then shift into a specific form of the issue. One presentation example stood out. Stereotypes, as us Appalachians know too well, are a critical way that outsiders make profit of the region, as scholars have noted.[2] The group of cadets took on the issue of stereotypes by examining the concept of redneck. This group of four students pulled up their presentation titled "Rednecks: The Backbone of Appalachia." During the process of working on group work, I guided the cadets primarily by helping them form research questions and not necessarily telling them where to find sources. To my memory, I never explained that rednecks were the backbone of the Appalachian region. It brought a smile to my face when I saw they came to this idea on their own.

There was discussion of ten thousand justice-seeking miners marching from Marmet to Mingo, West Virginia, in solidarity to protest the working conditions coal miners faced in the 1920s. Cadets eloquently articulated how the bandanna worn around the miners' necks were both practical in the sense that they were often worn as makeshift masks to keep out the coal dust or wipe sweat from their faces. But the students began to see how the bandanna was a symbol of unity that stretched across ethnicity and race, understood to represent those who were being oppressed by coal companies abusing their workers. Eventually the literacy matter of the red bandanna came to be a naming in the region. The students drew connections of how the word shifted from its initial usage into something more culturally pejorative in our American lexicon. They displayed a word web of sorts that connected *redneck* to other terms like *hillbilly, white trash*, or *trailer trash*. It is a social word, filled with rhetorical power to demean and point to the class difference.

Another element of their presentation focused on how, through their research, they found connections between rednecks' origins to a modern-day revival of empowerment. They explained to the class how in 2018, West Virginia teachers went on strike. Much like the coal miners who marched for just working rights, these Appalachian educators wore a red bandanna. The cadets were surprised to see how a word, a title, especially one frequented as an invective, could be reclaimed and empowering. It was "a reminder of ancestral labor struggle," they wrote in their presentation. In more national contexts, they were able to draw nuanced connections to media representation of the term *redneck*. They played the original ad for Mountain Dew, which aired in 1966. Grayscale cartoon characters played on the screen in front of the class: a man with a bucket hat, white beard, a single bottom tooth, overalls complete with patches, and one shoe without a toe box yells out, "*YAHoo*." He sips from a growler of what can be assumed to be moonshine but in this case is labeled *Mountain Dew*. Eventually he and another man, this time completely barefoot, chase a woman who dons nothing much but a frayed dress. "Mountain Dew will tickle your innards, 'cause there's a bang in every bottle," we hear as a class as the commercial pans out. Other media examples that were brought to our attention from the presenting group were *The Beverly Hillbillies* and *Duck Dynasty*, both of which rely on these tropes. The group juxtaposed the original meaning of *redneck* to the rebranding of the term for profit, in this instance to sell either soda or a TV show, demonstrating how students were sensitive to what it means to be an outsider peering into a culture. This is even the case when we are discussing different regions in our own country. This project helped the cadets understand and articulate the importance of thinking through difficult questions of representation and meaning, to acknowledge the complexities that surround how particular *things* affect our literacies of place.

Matters of Appalachia

By spending time with the things in Justin's closet pages back, it was my aim to articulate that when it comes to animate literacies, we have to not only think about speech acts and writing and reading but also see those actions as caught in a web of things, of matterings that enable literacy to come to life. There were several objects that I brought into my Appalachian Culture course for this very reason. My cadets could read and learn about Appalachian culture, but it wasn't enough. I made it a goal to bring Appalachian folxways into the classroom.

I'd like to highlight a deliberate move to replace the *k* in *folkways* with an *x* in my course description, as I've explained elsewhere.[3] But I'd like to expand on this rhetorical move. The respelling of the term disrupts what we may think of common knowledge that belongs to regular people in a region. To this end, it brings into question who *can* belong somewhere. And furthermore, who *isn't* considered for belonging? Its etymological roots are murky when it comes to its exact origins, but among them, they include "crowd" or "common people."[4] My kin use the word *folks* all the time: "Y'all folks ready?" "Those folks down the road." At minimum, when we think of folkways, I'd argue we're discussing the ways of living and being that are grounded in banal ins and outs of everyday life. I think of how my granny used to fry in her favorite skillet because of its seasoning. Or how my mom washes dishes only with a *warsh rag* because it cleans better. It's just the way things are done. Often, these ways are passed down by word of mouth via stories. My shift here to spelling it with an *x* disrupts us into examining ways of living that may be not otherwise considered. This queers and challenges us to think about how others may have folxways that go unacknowledged and unrecognized while giving those of us who aren't necessarily supposed to survive in Appalachia a means of telling our stories too.

When I began the section in my class on Appalachian folxways, I framed it in such a way. It was important that the cadets understand that folxways don't necessarily have clear genealogies. Which is to say, you may not necessarily understand where a practice in the region originates, and if you were to ask such questions, you may end up with an answer like *It's always been that way* or *It's how I was taught.* It was important to discuss with my students the trap that we can get caught in if we always accept this common knowledge. To that end, it was important, in the weeks leading up to our section on folxways, that we discussed the cultural knowledge and history of Indigenous and Black peoples who often shared their own culture with the settlers in the region. We discussed the material realities of their treatment, including the Iroquoian language spread throughout southern Appalachia and Cherokee lands. It was deliberate that we discussed the Indian Removal Act and the realities of the American government displacing an estimated sixteen thousand Cherokee in what would eventually be called the Trail of Tears. This led to a discussion on the Indian Citizens Act of 1924 and how eventually Indigenous material cultures would be commercialized into tourist attractions for the sake of economic gain after the Great Depression. You can still see this now as you traverse the interstates in places like eastern Tennessee, western North Carolina, and eastern Kentucky, where there are billboards advertising tourist shops of Native artifacts. I can even remember visiting these places as a child on our way down to Gatlinburg. Looking back at the mass production of dream catchers, drums, garish feathers attached to everything in the store, it fills me with unease. I wanted the cadets to realize that neoliberalism still carries over into the damage of Appalachia even today. It was made abundantly clear to the cadets that an entire semester could be devoted to Indigenous knowledge and history and that we could only begin to touch on the importance of those who lived with the land originally, in what we now refer to as Appalachia.

As another parallel to Indigenous wisdom impacting what we would consider folxways, we also spent time discussing Black Appalachians and their history in the region. It was a goal to complicate ideas of Blackness during the semester. Much like the commercial the students used in their project on the stereotypes of rednecks, the cadets and I discussed at length how Appalachia can wrongly be synonymous with the white body. We spent this week debunking that myth. Cadets learned that Black history, the Black Appalachian experience, and the history of Blackness in the region are still an ongoing effort. Black Appalachian histories are elided, and the efforts of Black Appalachian scholars are recovering and celebrating Black history. Cadets presented on Frank X Walker, and we examined the intersections of Affrilachia as a reclamation of identity. Looking at the work of such authors as William H. Turner, we spent time discussing the Mason-Dixon line and how West Virginia would eventually succeed from Virginia because they were on the side of God and not on the side of slavery—a topic we discussed at length too.[5] The cadets were shocked, I think, to learn slavery wasn't as simple as they perhaps had learned. We discussed that slavery existed in Appalachia but not to the extent it had in the Deep South. It was a surprising moment for the class to learn that the antislavery movement began in Appalachia, largely to the credit of the Quakers. I intentionally positioned these two sections—both concerning Indigenous history and the importance of Black Appalachians—before the segment on folxways. It stresses how knowledge comes from communities. I wanted to dispel the thinking that white Appalachians are solely responsible for the folx knowledge in the region; it's much more complicated than that.

The first literacy matter I brought to class was the banjo. We contextualized the object in the history of the slaves who were brought to Appalachian. I would be remiss as a Kentuckian if I didn't at least bring up the importance of music, especially bluegrass, and the banjo. We would even discuss flatfootin', and I told stories about how my nanny taught me flatfootin' as a child. To complicate this story, though, it was pertinent to explain that the banjo didn't come from Appalachia but would evolve to be Appalachian because of the knowledge brought here by slavery. This fact also being a matter of poverty—making music with minimal materials mattered. Race. Mattering. Music. Culture. It was all intertwined. It wasn't enough to simply discuss this information. Cadets needed to see it, hear it, be animated by it.

I invited Susan Pepper, an Appalachian musician, to Skype into our class and play for the cadets. She's been described as "authentic tradition-bearer, a cultural broker bridging the gap between generations of musicians past and present."[6] Susan lives in western North Carolina and grew up in Cincinnati to a family of Appalachian expats. Between performing her ballads and showing us a gourd banjo, a musical instrument that would resemble a banjo from Africa, she'd bring in conversations about Appalachian resistance. Ballads and songs and music coalesced around communities in Appalachia, she explained. She smartly connected racial identities and sound and material realities of Appalachia via her song, miles away in the mountains, where she was pickin' and grinnin' for an audience of cadets sitting on Cape Cod. It was a magical moment, one I don't think had ever happened at MMA with the Atlantic Ocean flowing right outside our classroom.

The *Foxfire* books are full of folxways, and excerpts were assigned for this portion of class.[7] *Foxfire* as an artifact of literacy is a fascinating text as a collection of oral histories; I was sure to contextualize for the students that folxways are propagated primarily through orality. Much like how Susan carried history in each strum of her banjo, folxways are primarily passed down in stories. The collection of essays that would come to be the first volume of *Foxfire* had a chapter on how soda ash left over from a wood stove, fireplace, or outside fire pit was used to make soap. So why not make soap with my students? I wasn't taught how to make soap directly from my relatives. My mom's mom used to tell me stories about how her family had to *warsh* their own clothes by hand and soap was hard to come by. It wasn't until the research in my graduate work that I began to experiment with making lye soap myself. I still do it to this day. It's a nice reminder of how you can transform the world around you, in this case some type of fat and lye solution, into materials we use without a second thought.

For this reason, I taught my students that folxways typically function and are sustained by four main modalities: through *stories*, through the act of *storytelling*, as *knowledge-making*, and are usually a matter of *survival*. I stressed that stories are things that take on lives of their own, that stories may differ from one holler to another—they're animate literacies. Perhaps they would have the same characters involved with minor plot points changing, depending on if you are on one side of a knob or a mountain versus another. Thus, who tells the story and how they tell it are important. When I asked the class who had sat around with their grandparents around the dinner table or the like and listened to stories about their family, most students raised their hands. Stories make us, with the process of storytelling being just as critical as the stories being told. This is how folx knowledge is sustained. Ultimately, too, folxways are a matter of survival. In a place like Appalachian, where literacy can still be a privilege, listening to and recalling stories were and still can be a matter of living and staying alive. Even something as simple as a bar of soap, an object we take for granted in modernity, was also a matter of surviving daily life for many Appalachians isolated by the landscape.

The specific day in class I brought in all the necessary materials to make soap with the cadets, I made sure to bring a story with me for a discussion about the material realities of folxways. We began class with the four principles I note above, but I also wanted to bring those four aspects to life. We discussed the log cabin and its design, how it was invented because of the physical environment and access to materials in the forests up and down

Appalachia. We discussed how the outhouse was and is sometimes still a necessity because of the remoteness of living on the land down in the mountains and region. There was a conversation about the moon door on wooden outhouses being a gendered remnant of Appalachia history too. Some of my distant family still to this day uses outhouses. In more modern contexts, though, I belong to communities that live in a co-op out in the foothills of Ohio, intentionally living off the grid. They use compostable toilets not because they can't afford plumbing but because they're making concerted efforts to live outside capitalistic systems and use permaculture as a means of living with the natural world.

We also discussed how moonshine, despite its appropriation to sell Mountain Dew, is a folxway too. Moonshiners are portrayed as criminals nowadays, and yes, distributing liquor unlicensed constitutes a crime but especially so during abolitionist times, the students learned. But it wasn't unusual to respect moonshiners in the local communities. A live-and-let-live mentality, you could say; shiners provided a service like anyone else and frequently hold reverence in the community. I told the students a story about how my maternal grandfather used to make 'shine. I didn't come from coal; I came from corn, at least on my mom's side. Every fall now that I'm grown, I go pick apples with my friends and family, and we make wine together, I explained to the cadets. Of course, I didn't go into details as to how to make it. Yet telling the story of homemade wine connects me to the stories of my ancestors, keeping the tradition alive. I can tell my reader, though, that the process of boiling the must, breaking down the apples and honey, of reaching into the trees and pulling down autumnal fruit years away from my grandfather keeps him alive. My mom still tells me how she'd go visit her father after he and Nanny got a divorce. He lit his single-wide trailer with oil lamps. Surely it smelled like cast-iron stove and ashen wood in the wintertime. My grandfather used to sip his white lightnin' and dance to records. My mom's tiny body would be spun around by her father, laughing and dancing to Jerry Lee Lewis. She told me once how the police came to his trailer, storming in and prying open the floorboards to reveal ball jars full of white *lick-ur*. I can imagine the cops swirling around the containers, the liquid sloshing with the consistency of oil. He went to prison many times for those bootleg bottles.

The day I made soap with my cadets, I also brought up an image of the ginseng on the projector. It was an opportunity to connect story and survival and its intersection with Indigenous knowledge. The root is sacred medicine in the region. The ginseng has deep roots in the history of the region. Smart work has expounded its import in detail, such as Luke Manget's book *Ginseng Diggers: A History of Root and Herb Gathering in Appalachia*.[8] That day in class, we discussed how it was a means of survival because it could be sold for profit, especially for poor families. That the settlers abused the knowledge passed down to them by Indigenous people, taking more than needed. Now the root is protected in certain federal areas and has led to interesting legal predicaments.[9] It was an opportunity to explain to the cadets that my great-grandfather, on my mom's mom's side, would scour the countryside looking for roots such as ginseng. Sure, it was abused and removed to excess, but it was still used among other herbs and barks to heal when there wasn't a doctor nearby. I remember that day, after I retold that story, I said out loud to the students, "That doesn't even sound real, does it?" Laughing, I realized that I was able to share my Appalachian literacies in new ways now. To close out class, as I mixed my lye solution with the coconut oil, I explained how these ingredients are vastly different from the tallow Appalachians would use over a century ago. And the organic sodium hydroxide I was using is a far cry from the soda ash that had to be collected from the gray ashy aftermath of many fires made to cook and heat by. There is a bar of soap from that class period that I put on my campus office shelf.

Finally, when it comes to the materiality of literacy in my course, as I've previously mentioned, I taught two texts in the class: *What You Are Getting Wrong about Appalachia* and the novel *The Prettiest Star*. While a shorter read, Catte's text made me nervous. Working at an institution that has a reputation for having some vocal Trump supporters, a polemic against Appalachia being Trump country could easily go awry. It was toward the end of the semester, and cadets were vying for summer (our spring semester runs into June), so assigning a book at the end of a long semester may have not been the best decision on my part. To be frank, I'm not sure most of the cadets read the book. However, one way that it did find its way into the class was the group project that I've already discussed. The group that researched issues of criminality discussed the prison industrial complex, a topic that Catte spends a considerable amount of time with in her text. The group brought up the documentary *13th*, which premiered on Netflix in 2016—early in the Trumpian years.[10] The film details the harrowing American realities of the Thirteenth Amendment of the Constitution, which makes way for modern slavery via the prison industry in our country. The group was making connections between Catte's argument that Appalachia, much as coal companies exploited the land, is now selling property to the prison industrial complex for pipedreams of economic revival and the racial injustices that Black Americans face. The students were making complex, deeply human connections about race, economics, justice, and Appalachia. I was impressed that the cadets would integrate such politicized topics into their presentations considering our sometimes political campus. It was a very proud moment I had watching students articulate difficult truths.

Carter Sickels's novel *The Prettiest Star* can easily take a reader and shred their heart into pieces. A harrowing story of Appalachian queerness, it beautifully haunted me for months after I first read it. Then reread it. Then wrote on it, then taught it. There was a vast number of cadets who came up to me many times that semester to tell me they rarely read novels, but they read it in one clean swipe. What's perhaps the most rewarding part of teaching with the book was that our provost approved funding for Carter Sickles to do a reading of his novel for the campus. While it was a virtual visit, many cadets in my courses showed up. It was advertised on campus through the Office of Intercultural Engagement, and the president welcomed Carter at the beginning of the session. Cadets made connections, asking questions about sexuality, Appalachia, writing, and reading. The novel offered synthesis, I think, for the cadets. There is a gap between picking up a hard copy of a book, the thing itself, and reading, bringing to life the words on the page, and the person who created the book. The affective literacies of reading, teaching, and writing about a novel and the material realities of the novel being circulated in a class accumulated into one of the sincerest ways for me as a teacher. Appalachia became alive in ways that I hadn't anticipated for me during Sickles's reading. It reminds me that Appalachian literacies matters can live on through the stories we tell and the things we use to tell those stories with, affecting us even miles away from the places we carry with us.

Rednecks in the Commonwealth

In my stint being on the Steering Committee for the Appalachian Studies Association, it wasn't unusual to see fellow millennials and Gen Zs moving through the halls at the conference site wearing the infamous red bandanna. "I wear this because I want to resist the stereotypes," a young participant told me once at the Cincinnati conference in 2018 after we held a panel on queer Appalachia. The familiar red paisley print was tied around her neck. I thought of that moment when I stood in front of my class and declared, in a manner of speaking, *We wouldn't have unions if it wasn't for rednecks.*

Of course, we can give credit to Patrick Huber's "Red Necks and Red Bandanas" for doing the critical historic work of connecting union labor, Appalachia, and coal miners to the red bandanna.[11] We read Huber's article in class. And the week we were reading about rednecks, debunking the common mistake that those who worked in the field had red, sunburnt necks at the end of the day, we also were engaging with the Coal Mine Wars. That part of the schedule was memorable. We split into group work and created a timeline of the events leading up to the Coal Mine Wars, beginning with Cabin Creek and Paint Creek, then the Battle of Matewan, and finally Blair Mountain. The students were to piece together a timeline of events, highlighting key moments and individuals that would eventually lead to the largest insurrection since the Civil War. We watched the hundred-year anniversary memorial video that took place in 2021 at Blair Mountain, West Virginia. The students were connecting history to the aftereffects of labor movements, a hundred years later. Teaching at a unionized institution such as MMA, having a number of cadets who come from union families, something began to click for me. These are the teaching moments I cherish the most—the ones where the teacher and student work together to think differently, to see the world anew. They're rare, I think, and have only happened organically for me. My students in their investigation of coalmining debacles taught me something about being Appalachian in a state so far away from Kentucky and West Virginia. I wasn't raised in a union family. But now I was unionized, which had its connection to home.

There's a sense of union pride in Massachusetts. The Massachusetts Teaching Association, frequently referred to as MTA, is a juggernaut of educational prowess and is the umbrella organization for roughly four hundred associations in Massachusetts. When tenure track began on September 1 back in 2019, I couldn't have explained what a CBA was—a collective bargaining agreement—and I certainly could not have explained why it was referenced all over campus. Only later would I learn about a collective bargaining agreement and that it dictated protections, limitations, salaries, credits, labor—my livelihood. When I signed my contract with MMA, human resources wasn't there to explain much beyond that I would belong to MSCA, the Massachusetts State College Association. No one in graduate school explained what bargaining is or how a CBA protects you.

No one explained how such a dense document, full of legalese, wordy definitions, and circular citations, can mediate your entire career. As literacy material, I was quite ignorant of how the document made up my job and how it would shape my eventual future as the president of our MMA chapter.

The spring I taught Appalachia Cultures, I also ran for our local union chapter as president and won. Did I know much about unions? No, but my students inspired me through the learning we did together in class. Three years was enough to become familiar with the governing document, our CBA that shaped the faculty's workload. Maybe it was naive of me to run for the highest rank in the chapter because the students in class were learning about unions. It was certainly an unexpected turn but one that I am confessing to for the first time here: it was because my students in Appalachian class had taught me to connect to Appalachia in new ways, even when I don't seem to find myself in the shadow of the rolling knobs of my childhood.

Home as Movable

An animated understanding of literacy recognizes literacy as a force—it moves its actors; as performative—we do literacy; as sensational—we come to touch, smell, embody meaning; as caught up in an eddy of humans and nonhumans—these are words, there is a page, you are holding *something*; always flowing in particular places to shape meaning—where you are sculpts your understanding of the world. Moving away from the Appalachian region to an entirely different part of the country has only made this definition come even more alive. I intentionally began this final chapter with the details of the Cape Cod Canal. In its existence, we find an apt metaphor for the closing of *Reading, Writing, and Queer Survival*: the canal is a current, a nonhuman actor that has shaped the cumulation of this project in the same way that my papaw's hillside did, similar to Justin's water heater or Lexi's monstrous metaphors. The canal shapes our campus, our curriculum, our experiences as faculty for our students. The first-year students even have a day that they all look forward to in their initial year, of waking up at 5:00 a.m. to be hurried to the campus beach and plunge into the canal, a maritime baptism of sorts. I'm reassured of its tradition, that it is not required but a rite of passage. I can't help but think they're learning to be literate in ways that are unique to the Cape. They aren't learning in the ways Lara did on her campus nestled in the bluegrass of Kentucky. I listen to the stories of the cadets in my classes, of the regiment, of the long night watches on the ship that are mandatory for license majors. They show up in uniforms. Their stories are unique *because* of the ocean that washes up against our university. There are ways of being on campus that still fascinate me as an Appalachian so far away from home.

But just as the canal flows up and down, altering directions but retaining its shape, its function, its striking beauty, I realize that home begins to move, too, when you listen to the land and you listen to its literacies.

During the last day of my Appalachian Cultures course, I drove this point home. Our Appalachian queen Dolly Parton's 2014 song "Home" seemed like a great way to wrap up our class. Dolly details a home we Appalachians know so well. In my last bit of reflection for the class, it was difficult to fight back tears. There was a fierce vulnerability in being able to share stories about the Kentucky that made me. It never occurred to me that I would be able to pass on generational knowledge about folxways, about my great-granddad Saylor being a root worker in the hills, about how to make soap from soda ash, about the history of hillbillies, of coal, of banjos, of the actual American struggles down home in Appalachia—to make this my career. The class period was short; I'd never cried before in class. Surely, a June-day tear welled up as the sea reflected the sunlight on the canal. I explained to the cadets something to the effect of, *I am immensely proud of each of you for the respect and openness you came to class with. This class was special to me because it reminded me of where*

I called home, but unexpectedly, you all are helping me make this place home too. Yet I think all Appalachians can navigate home in unusual ways, can be night-crowlers, because here I am crawling through the country in ways that don't always make sense, of the earth and hillside yet drawn to water, carrying the mountains to the sea.

Acknowledgments

In making room for matter, the queer, feelings and affects, place, and especially for the nonhumans, my acknowledgments here must break with the conventional genre.

This book, as with most academics' first manuscript, began as a dissertation. When I first started this project, I erected an altar next to my desk, built as a reminder of the spiritual and physical labor I poured into these pages. On it sat images of my ancestors: my soulmate and first fur baby, Mocah, a long-hair calico who passed when I was seventeen; Papaw, my dad's dad, who I write about in the prologue; and my aunt Jadene, who whispered to me as she lay dying when I was nine years old, "Stay in school, Caleb." *I've never left*, I tell her some days, looking at her smiling face when I feel discouraged. Papaw, Jadene, and Mocah have stayed with me during this entire book, and for that I'm grateful.

There was a vase on my altar full of small stones. I'd collect one rock for every job application while I was on the market—one pebble equaling one application; there are about seventy pebbles. Of those near-hundred stones, I found a tenure-track position at Massachusetts Maritime Academy. I was able to land my tenure-track position because of many people. Among them, Dr. J. Palmeri. They have been a mentor in all the ways a mentor should be and more—what J. has given me in over a decade of mentorship is much more than many academics receive in their careers, even their lifelong friendships. Over the many hours of meetings, conversations, and draft after draft after draft, we laughed, and they listened to me cry. I was lucky to run Miami University's Composition Program with them, which taught me invaluable lessons about pedagogy, writing, and being human in the academy. They have been an indispensable academic drag mother of sorts, but more than that, they have been a friend. I wouldn't be where I am at in my life if not for J. Thank you, J., for seeing the best in me when I couldn't. I pray the Haus of Palmeri continues to change the world.

At Mass. Maritime, I have encountered several colleagues and administrators who enabled this project to move forward. To my colleagues Dr. Jenna Morton-Aiken and Dr. Sarah Moon, I give my thanks for being collaborative and running our Writing Program together. Provost Pavilions and Dean McKenna have supported the launch of this project and encouraged me to give talks across the country. And perhaps more indirectly, I want to thank my dear friends on campus Dr. Mike Gutierrez and Pamela Cerrud-Ahern. They gifted plenty of laughs, and there are memories we've made that I'll always hold dear. Dr. Nelson Ritschel, who implored me to reach out to the University Press of Kentucky, has been an unwavering anchor in what, at times, could be considered a maelstrom. He is the type of academic that you want on your side—ambitious, calculating, and brilliant—and he has enabled me to arrive at a place of confidence in my career where risk-taking and facing fears have become empowering and freeing. Thank you, Nelson.

Thinking back to the origins of *Reading, Writing, and Queer Survival*, my graduate mentors come to mind. Michele Simmons guided me along my path of person-based research and helped me pass my IRB. Dr. Emily Legg taught me the importance of story and being a storyteller. Dr. Roxanne Ornelas has always been welcoming as my outside reader, and I share her valuation of place. Even though she joined later in my journey of writing the first drafts, Dr. Sara Webb-Sunderhaus and her essential

Acknowledgments

work on literacies and Appalachia have been indispensable in this project. My gratitude to these folks can't be fully expressed in words.

On my dissertation altar, I had three small ceramic replicas of my other fur babies, Kali, Zeus, and Oya. They wrote this book with me from start to finish. As I type this now, they are near. Zeus asleep, regal-like, in the top of their kitty tower. Queen Kali basking in the sunlight. Oya, with her unrelenting devotion, passed tragically in my arms in the summer of 2020. She was the most loyal familiar I've ever had in this incarnation around the sun. I think I see her sometimes, tail plumed and mostly fur, meeting me when I open the door arriving home and her small mews echoing from the other side. Oya, I miss you, and I thank you still. I wouldn't be here if it weren't for my cats. They've offered companionship in some of my more dire, depressive states. They allow me to care for them, and in that kinship, I know that I have the opportunity to put love into this world. They've supported me in writing this project in so many ways.

I collected pieces of Appalachian coal too: glossy and fractured, they used to sit on the altar. The coal reminds me of time, of how time works in the mountains—slow and powerful, the coal formed after years like the stories I collected from participants. This dissertation belongs to the coal and the participants as much as it belongs to me. Justin, Lexi, Elizabeth, Macy, and Lara—along with the other participants whose stories didn't get to make it in because of the constrained time I had in writing this project—I appreciate you and your words. In some ways, your stories taught me more about literacy, writing, and the power of language than any graduate education could. This dissertation was written with you and because of you.

Every time I sit down to write, I light a candle. It's said our reverence for fire and smoke is in our DNA, inborn from our ability to cook. Fire is deeply connected with the human condition, and I want to express thanks to the fire that burned on my altar year round. Its flame was a reminder of the passion I have for the work I do and am dedicated to continuing. Fire also represents the hearth and community; we gather around fire for warmth and communion. Celebrations are marked by pyres. I've danced around many upstretched blazes in the process of this book to honor the flames like my ancestors burned ages ago. Fire provides for our families all these things.

My queer family has been like that flame, burning endlessly in their support of me and this project. Kyle, my queer brother, best friend, my Meredith Grey to his Cristina Yang, listened to me over uncountable phone calls, Facetimed for hours while he chain-smoked, and I'd ramble on about literacy, posthumanist ideals, and new materialism. When I didn't know how I was going to make it to my job interviews, he told me, "Bitch, come on. We're gonna drive this car like we stole it." I live on the ocean because Kyle shared the drive to Cape Cod when I couldn't do it alone. Sometimes queer families move and morph, and despite being hundreds of miles away in the mountains, Travis, you were there during the earlier drafts. He once said that words could hardly express how I helped him in writing his first book; I'd like to echo his words here. Thank you, Travis, for helping me understand the benefits of compromise and how to stand up for myself when I needed to put myself first.

My mom, Twana, has been and always will be an immovable mountain of support in my life. I cannot count all the ways she has helped me in writing *Reading, Writing, and Queer Survival*. I would send her drafts to read, and she'd eagerly in her own way tell me feedback and her thoughts. It's rare to have a parent so willing to help their child as much as my mom has and continues to do today. My mom has saved my life, and there is no way to repay her for her kindness and understanding. Indubitably, Mom is a warrior who taught me that when the world tells you that you can't, you make sure to do anything in your power to do it anyways. The reason I am able to write through pain and trauma, about the mountains and land, and see the power and agency that the world around us has is because of her. I owe her my life.

To my other queer family members: I must say thank you a million times over to Dr. Tonya Krouse. How can I repay the many nights of dancing to Prince, the bottles of wine, and spilling tea? I can't. I thank you for helping me reaching this point. Jimmy, thank you for always reminding me of my tenacity and perseverance. Your enduring optimism and candor have sustained me in ways unnamed. I give gratitude to others as well: Emily, Chase, Mandy, Bridget, and Hua. This project wouldn't have been possible either without the help of Miami University's English Department. I wouldn't have been able to travel to Appalachia, collect stories and meet queer storytellers, or find a job in merely four years. I want to thank Sarah, Denise, Rachel, Dr. Detloff, Dr. Mao, and Dr. Dunning. To Abby Freeland, I want to extend a personal thanks because you have been a rudder in some more doubtful times I've swam through. You have helped this project come to life, and I can't be more appreciative. Ashley Runyon and the others at the University Press of Kentucky, I am grateful for everyone seeing the light in not only this project but future possibilities too.

I have two final notes of appreciation. I want to thank the Indiana squirrel who kept me company during the summer of 2018 as I read and researched and wrote. We fought each other around our backyard. You ate my tanning lotion, stole my outdoor prayer flags, and chased me in the house. As I read book after book and uncountable articles, you always kept a watchful eye from above in your great oak tree. You sponsored this book as much as anyone and anything. And to the Cape Cod Canal, you showed me that when there isn't supposed to be a way, and despite humanity's seemingly unrelenting aim at challenging the land, how there can be beauty in a world that isn't supposed to exist.

Appendix

Interview Questions and Consent Form

Interview Questions

- ❖ Trauma:
  - ➢ How would you describe your sexual identity? Sexual orientation?
  - ➢ How would you define trauma? What is trauma to you?
  - ➢ Have you experienced any trauma in relationship to your queerness?
  - ➢ Does this trauma have any impact with growing up in Appalachia?
  - ➢ What are you able of telling about the trauma you experienced?
  - ➢ What reactions did you have to this experience, both then and now? Emotionally? Physically?
  - ➢ What was the most difficult part of this experience? What is unforgettable?
  - ➢ Looking back, what do you believe you learned from your experience?
  - ➢ Have you considered that trauma played a major role in your life? Why?

- Do you see trauma playing a role in other queer people's lives in Appalachia? Could you give me some examples?
- Do you have anything else you would like to add about your experiences in Appalachia? Any other stories that you find important to share?
- If you could offer advice for others who find themselves in/with similar experiences, what would you say?
- Would you consider trauma important in learning to read and write?
- How does reading and writing factor into literacy for you?

❖ Body:
- How would you describe your relationship with your body?
- How does being queer affect your body?
- How is your understanding of your body affected by being in Appalachia?
- Would you say that your body is read as queer?
- Has your body ever been threatened because of your queerness? If so, how?
- How do you experience your queerness through your body?
- Does your body limit you in any way?
- In general, how do you talk about your body?
- When you were learning to read, how did your body play a role?
- Were you read to when you were young? If so, where (e.g., before bed)?

❖ Place:
- What part of Appalachia are you from?
- What relationship do you have with Appalachia? Would you call it home?
- Do you identify as Appalachian? If so, when did you know you were Appalachian?

- In regard to your sexual orientation, could you tell me your experience being queer* in Appalachia? This can include your coming-out story, if you have come out. If so, was it in Appalachia? If not, why? How did you know you were queer?
- Are there any places that are unique to your area? If so, how did these places affect your understanding of where you grew up / lived?
- Are there any LGBTQ-friendly places in your area / where you lived? Are there any unsafe places or places to avoid if you are LGBTQ+?
- Where did you learn to read and write?
- Did your particular school play a role in your reading/writing?
- Do you have any favorite local authors?
- Was your place of education important in learning to read and write?

❖ Spirituality:
- Please talk about your religious upbringing. For example, did you participate in organized religion (e.g., go to church, synagogue, temple, or mosque), celebrate holidays, and/or contribute time or funds to faith-based organizations or causes?
- What role has religion played in your life?
- Please describe the development of your religious identity. In what ways has it changed over time?
- What age were you when individuals within your faith community knew you were LGBTQ+? What was the process in which they learned about it?
- What motivated you to come out within your faith community when and how you did?
- How did you coming out impact your relationship with members of the faith community?
- Have your religious/faith views changed over time, and if so, how?

- Were any changes in your perspectives about faith influenced by experiences related to you being LGBTQ+?
- Was there a particular person or persons in your faith community who was a positive influence on your faith experiences?
- Relevant to the intersection of your faith and being LGBTQ+, who was the most significant individual?
- What are your favorite memories of an event or events in your experiences in your faith community?
- Have there been moments or experiences that have positively reinforced your LGBTQ+ identity within the context of faith-based experiences?
- What is a negative memory of an event or events in your experiences in your faith community? Can you describe a time when you felt excluded or othered in a faith-based setting because of an LGBTQ+ identity?
- What impact do you think being LGBTQ+ had within the faith communities you have been part of?
- What would you consider to be your greatest challenges of being LGBTQ+ in the context of your faith community?
- How has your LGBTQ+ identity influenced your faith-based experiences in general or specific examples?
- What insights or advice would you have for LGBTQ+ individuals who want to be active in their faith communities?

Consent Form: Animate Literacies

My name is Caleb Pendygraft, and I'm currently a PhD candidate in Miami University of Ohio's English Department. I'm a queer pagan from Appalachia Kentucky doing research on the literacy of other Appalachian queers. My research is moving away from more traditional studies of literacy that understand literacy to be merely reading and writing. Instead, I'm looking

Appendix

at other ways queers in Appalachia "read" and "write" themselves into their world. I am collecting stories from participants that look at four areas in their lives: trauma, their body, places in Appalachia, and religious/spiritual communities they have belonged or do belong to. Are you from Appalachia? Do you identify as queer—including lesbian, gay, bisexual, trans*, into kink/leather or fetish, and/or any other way you may identify with queerness? I'd love to hear your story.

I am collecting stories in a number of ways, including collecting video interviews and documentation of significant places in Appalachia that hold value to you. In the instance that you would like to participate in the video documentation, I'd be happy to travel to you if I'm able—especially if you're near southern Ohio or Kentucky. However, you *do not* have to participate in video documentation if you'd prefer not to. We can interview in person, over the phone, or even through Skype. I will use a series of interview questions as a set of guidelines to collect your narrative, with the aim of having a conversation and listening to your narrative. The video and/or audio interviews will also be used in writing my dissertation, along with conferences, presentations, and publications. The video footage will be stored on an encrypted hard drive. My dissertation committee and myself would be the only ones to access this data before it is used in the dissertation, publications, or conference presentations. By letting you speak your own story, it's my hope our work together will broaden how literacy is studied for LGBTQ+ folks in Appalachia.

You may choose to complete an audio-recorded interview that I will then transcribe, or you may choose to conduct a video-recorded interview. However, if you choose to be videoed, be aware that your face may be shown in any digital online publications that arise from this research. Your name and any names associated with your stories can be changed. Any personal information will not be linked to your video interview (e.g., address, income, job, etc.) without your permission.

Since trauma is one of the areas I focus on, I ask that you only participate if your experience of trauma in your narrative is no less than two years prior to our interview. This way, risk is reduced in having to relive the trauma events. In the telling of your narrative, you may reexperience some traumatic flashbacks. It is up to you whether to continue or to withdraw from the interviewing process if you find this occurring. I have included resources at the end of the consent form that may be useful if you were to experience such distress. The video and quotations will be used with your permission, and I will share the video and writing with you before finalization of the data.

You can withdraw from the study at any point by letting me know that you would not want to participate in person or any other means of contacting me. You may choose not to answer specific questions but continue to participate if you like. I will share all writing and edited video from your data with you before publishing it and will make any changes you request. If at any time you feel misrepresented or that for some reason my writing about our time together is misconstruing your story, you have the right to withdraw from the study.

If you agree to participate in this research, "Animate Literacies," please sign below, detach the signature section, and return to us. Please keep the information above for future reference. By signing, you agree that you are at least 18 years old.

_____   _____
Participant Name (Printed)   Date

_____   _____
Participant Name (Signed)   Date

- I agree to an interview that will be audio recorded and then transcribed; quotes from the transcript may be used in print and digital publications.

Appendix

- I agree to a video-recorded interview; edited portions of the video may appear in online publications, in my electronic dissertation, and in online journals.
- I would NOT like my name used in this study and will be referred to by a pseudonym in any publications. I understand that if I agree to be video recorded, I may still be recognizable to people who know me even if I use a pseudonym.
- I am OK with my real name being used in relation to quotes from or edited video from my interview.

Resources

Gay, Lesbian, Bisexual, and Transgender National Hotline: 1-888-843-4564

Trans Lifeline: 1-877-565-8860

The Trevor Project: 1-866-488-7386

Notes

Prologue

1. Deborah Brandt, *Literacy in American Lives* (Cambridge, MA: Cambridge University Press, 2001), 19.
2. Mel Chen, *Animacies: Biopolitics, Racial Mattering, and Queer Affect* (Durham, NC: Duke University Press, 2012), 2.
3. Donna Haraway, *Staying with the Trouble: Making Kin in the Chthulucene* (Durham, NC: Duke University Press, 2016), 55.
4. Digital Archive of Literacy Narratives, accessed August 1, 2023, https://www.thedaln.org/#/home; Krista Bryson, "The Literacy Myth in the Digital Archive of Literacy Narratives," *Computers and Composition* 29, no. 3 (2012): 254–68; Deborah Brandt, *The Rise of Writing: Redefining Mass Literacy* (Cambridge, MA: Cambridge University Press, 2014); Cynthia L. Selfe and Gail E. Hawisher, *Literate Lives in the Information Age: Narratives of Literacy from the United States* (Mahwah, NJ: Lawrence Erlbaum Associates, 2004).
5. Casey Boyle, *Rhetoric as a Posthuman Practice* (Columbus: The Ohio State University Press, 2018); Laurie Gries, *Still Life with Rhetoric: A New Materialist Approach for Visual Rhetorics* (Logan: Utah State University Press, 2015); Scot Barnett and Casey Boyle, eds., *Rhetoric, through Everyday Things* (Tuscaloosa: The University of Alabama Press, 2016); Bruce Latour, *Reassembling the Social: An Introduction to Actor-Network Theory* (Oxford: Oxford University Press, 2007); Laura Micciche, *Doing Emotion* (Portsmouth, NH: Boynton/Cook, 2007); Micciche, "Staying with Emotion," *Composition Forum* 34, (Summer 2016); Amy Propen, *Visualizing Posthuman*

Conservation in the Age of the Anthropocene (Columbus: The Ohio State University Press, 2018).

6. Candance Kuby, Karen Spector, and Jaye Johnson Thiel, eds., *Posthumanism and Literacy Education: Knowing/Becoming/Doing Literacies* (New York: Routledge, 2019), 2.

7. Ibid.

8. Ibid.

9. Ibid., 4.

10. Elizabeth Catte, *What You Are Getting Wrong about Appalachia* (Cleveland: Belt Publishing, 2017); Kim Donehower, Charlotte Hogg, and Eileen Schell, *Rural Literacies* (Carbondale: Southern Illinois University Press, 2007); Amanda Hayes, *The Politics of Appalachian Rhetoric* (Morgantown: West Virginia University Press, 2018); Sara Webb-Sunderhaus and Kim Donehower, *Rereading Appalachia: Literacy, Place, and Cultural Resistance* (Lexington: University Press of Kentucky, 2015).

11. Kevin Leander and Gail Boldt, "Rereading 'A Pedagogy of Multiliteracies': Bodies, Texts, and Emergence," *Journal of Literacy Research* 45, no. 1 (2013): 41.

12. Robert McRuer, *Crip Theory: Cultural Signs of Queerness and Disability* (New York: New York University Press, 2006).

13. Jeffrey Grabill, "Community-Based Research and the Importance of a Research Stance," *Writing Studies Research in Practice: Methods and Methodologies* (2012): 211.

14. See Martin Manalansan, "The 'Stuff' of Archives: Mess, Migration, and Queer Lives" *Radical History Review* 120 (2014): 94–107.

15. Cynthia Selfe (Emerita, The Ohio State University) gave a keynote talk to the Research Network Forum in spring 2015 in Tampa, Florida, for the Conference on College Composition and Communication.

1. Animacy, Literacy, and Queer Agency

1. Chen, *Animacies*; Michael Silverstein, "Hierarchy of Features and Ergativity," in *Grammatical Categories in Australian Languages*, ed. Robert M. W. Dixon (Canberra: Australian National University), 112–71.

2. Chen, *Animacies*, 24, 78.

3. Ibid., 2.

4. Ibid., 3.

5. Ibid., 4, 5.

6. Ibid., 11.

7. Ibid., 11.

8. Ibid., 58.

9. Ibid., 58.

10. J. Halberstam, "The Brandon Archive," in *In a Queer Time and Place: Transgender Bodies, Subcultural Lives* (New York: New York University Press, 2005), 22–46; Halberstam, *The Queer Art of Failure* (Durham, NC: Duke University Press, 2011); Annamarie Jagose, *Queer Theory: An Introduction* (New York: New York University Press, 1996); Sara Ahmed, *The Cultural Politics of Emotion* (New York: Routledge, 2004); Sara Ahmed, *Queer Phenomenology: Orientations, Objects, Others* (Durham, NC: Duke University Press, 2006).

11. Halberstam, *The Queer Art of Failure*; Manalansan, "The 'Stuff' of Archives"; Caroline Dadas, "Messy Methods: Queer Methodological Approaches to Research Social Media," *Computers and Composition* 40 (2016): 60–72; Heather Love, *Feeling Backward: Loss and the Politics of Queer History* (Cambridge, MA: Harvard University Press, 2007); Judith Butler, *Undoing Gender* (New York: Routledge, 2004), 19; Jose Muñoz, *Disidentifications: Queers of Color and the Performance of Politics* (Minneapolis: University of Minnesota, 1999); Stacey Waite, *Teaching Queer: Radical Possibilities for Writing and Knowing* (Pittsburgh, PA: University of Pittsburgh Press, 2017).

12. Chen, *Animacies*, 30.

13. Diana Coole and Samantha Frost, *New Materialisms: Ontology, Agency, and Politics* (Durham, NC: Duke University Press, 2010); Manuel DeLanda, *Assemblage Theory* (Edinburgh: Edinburgh University Press, 2016); Gries, *Still Life*.

14. *Merriam-Webster Dictionary*, "literate," accessed August 1, 2023, https://www.merriam-webster.com/dictionary/literate.

15. Jacqueline Jones Royster, *Traces of a Stream: Literacy and Social Change among African American Women* (Pittsburgh, PA: University of Pittsburgh Press, 2000), 45.

16. Ibid.

17. Ibid., 46.

18. Brian Street, "The New Literacy Studies," in *Cross-Cultural Approaches to Literacy*, ed. Brian Street (London: Cambridge University Press, 1993), 432.

19. Harvey Graff, *The Literacy Myth: Literacy and Social Structure in the Nineteenth-Century City* (New York: Academic Press, 1982), 8.

20. J. Elspeth Stuckey, *The Violence of Literacy* (Portsmouth, NH: Boynton/Cook, 1991), 18.

21. Walter Mignolo, *The Darker Side of the Renaissance: Literacy, Territoriality, and Colonization* (Ann Arbor, MI: University of Michigan Press, 2003), 45.

22. Ibid., 6.

23. Deborah Brandt, "Sponsors of Literacy," *College Composition and Communication* 49, no. 2 (1998): 166.

24. To reach this metric, I searched for "Deborah Brandt" in GoogleScholar.

25. Kara Poe Alexander, "Reciprocal Literacy Sponsorship in Service-Learning Settings," *Literacy in Composition Studies* 5, no. 1 (2017): 21–48, https://doi.org/10.21623/1.5.1.3.

26. Brandt, "Sponsors," 166–67.

27. Ibid., 168.

28. Sometimes a text can be seen as a sponsor, but the agency is still usually attributed to the people who wrote it. See Kuby, Spector, and Theil's introduction to *Posthumanism and Literacy Education* for more on this.

29. Lisa Mastrangelo, "Community Cookbooks: Sponsors of Literacy and Community Identity," *Community Literacy Journal* 10, no. 1 (2015): 73–86, https://doi.org/10.1353/clj.2015.0021; Marcy L. Galbreath, "Sponsors of Agricultural Literacies: Intersections of Institutional and Local Knowledge in a Farming Community," December 30, 2015, https://muse.jhu.edu/article/605293/pdf; Ciaran B. Trace, "Information in Everyday Life: Boys' and Girls' Agricultural Clubs as Sponsors of Literacy, 1900–1920," *Information and Culture* 49, no. 3: 265–93; Mike P. Cook and Ryle Frey, "Using Superheroes to Visually and Critically Analyze Comics, Stereotypes, and Society," *SANE Journal: Sequential Art Narrative in Education* 2, no. 2 (2017).

30. Sara Webb-Sunderhaus, "A Family Affair: Competing Sponsors of Literacy in Appalachian Students' Lives," *Community Literacy Journal* 2, no. 1 (2007): 6–7, https://doi.org/10.25148/clj.2.1.009502.

31. Alexander, "Reciprocal Literacy Sponsorship in Service-Learning Settings," 22.

32. Ann M. Lawrence, "Literacy Narratives as Sponsors of Literacy: Past Contributions and New Directions for Literacy-Sponsorship Research," *Curriculum Inquiry* 45, no. 3 (2015): 304–29, https://doi.org/10.1080/03626784.2015.1031058.

33. Deborah Brandt and Katie Clinton, "Limits of the Local: Expanding Perspectives on Literacy as a Social Practice," *Journal of Literacy Research* 34, no. 3 (2002): 337–56, https://doi.org/10.1207/s15548430jlr3403_4.

34. Ibid., 338.

35. Ibid., 346.

36. Ibid., 348.

37. Ahmed, *Cultural Politics*.

38. Kuby, Spector, and Thiel, *Posthumanism and Literacy Education*, 14.

Notes to Pages 10–14

39. Karen Michelle Barad, *Meeting the Universe Halfway: Quantum Physics and the Entanglement of Matter and Meaning* (Durham, NC: Duke University Press, 2007); Jane Bennett, *Vibrant Matter: A Political Ecology of Things* (Durham, NC: Duke University Press, 2010).

40. Clay Walker, "Composing Agency: Theorizing the Readiness Potentials of Literacy Practices," *Literacy in Composition Studies* 3, no. 2 (2015): 1–21, https://doi.org/10.21623/1.3.2.2.

41. Kenneth Burke, *A Grammar of Motives* (Berkeley: University of California Press, 1974).

42. Marilyn Cooper, "Rhetorical Agency as Emergent and Enacted," *College Composition and Communication* 62, no. 3 (2011): 420–49, http://www.jstor.org/stable/27917907.

43. Arabella Lyon, *Deliberative Acts: Democracy, Rhetoric, and Rights* (University Park: Pennsylvania State University Press, 2013), 97.

44. Mollie Blackburn, "Exploring Literacy Performances and Power Dynamics at the Loft: 'Queer Youth Reading the World and the Word,'" *Research in the Teaching of English* (2003): 467–90; Mollie Blackburn and Katherine Schultz, *Interrupting Hate: Homophobia in Schools and What Literacy Can Do about It* (New York: Teachers College Press, 2015); Zan Meyer Gonçalves, *Sexuality and the Politics of Ethos in the Writing Classroom* (Carbondale: Southern Illinois University Press, 2005); Harriet Malinowitz, *Textual Orientations: Lesbian and Gay Students and the Making of Discourse Communities* (Portsmouth, NH: Boynton/Cook, 1995).

45. Eric Darnell Pritchard, *Fashioning Lives: Black Queers and the Politics of Literacy* (Carbondale: Southern Illinois University Press, 2017), 38.

46. Paulo Freire and Donaldo Macedo, *Literacy: Reach the Word and the World* (South Hadley, MA: Bergin & Garvey, 1987), 58–59.

47. Ibid., 35.

48. Gries, *Still Life*, 57.

49. Ahmed, *Queer Phenomenology*, 25–28.

50. Ibid., 67.

51. Ibid., 188.

52. Halberstam, *Queer Art*, 2–3.

53. Adrienne Rich, "Compulsory Heterosexuality and Lesbian Existence," *Signs: Journal of Women in Culture and Society* 5, no. 4 (1980): 631–60, https://doi.org/10.1086/493756.

54. Chen, *Animacies*, 233.

55. James Paul Gee, "Literacy, Discourse, and Linguistics: Introduction *and* What Is Literacy?" in Ellen Cushman et al., eds., *Literacy: A Critical Sourcebook* (Boston: Bedford/St. Martin's, 2001), 526, 529.

56. Ibid., 527.
57. Ibid., 527.
58. Ibid., 528.
59. Ibid., 526, 529.
60. David Wallace and Jonathan Alexander, "Queer Rhetorical Agency: Questioning Narratives of Heteronormativity," *JAC* 29, no. 4 (2009), 793–819.
61. Ibid., 799.
62. Ibid., 800.
63. Ibid., 800.
64. Waite, *Teaching Queer*, 126.
65. Jonathan Alexander, *Literacy, Sexuality, Pedagogy Theory and Practice for Composition Studies* (Logan: Utah State University Press, 2008).
66. Ibid., 3, 5.
67. Waite, *Teaching Queer*, 126.
68. Ibid., 131.
69. Donehower, Hogg, and Schell, *Rural Literacies*, 4.
70. Waite, *Teaching Queer*, 132.
71. Ibid., 137.
72. Robert McRuer, *Crip Theory: Cultural Signs of Queerness and Disability* (New York: New York University Press, 2006).
73. Shirley Brice Heath, *Ways with Words: Language, Life and Work in Communities and Classrooms* (Cambridge, NY: Cambridge University Press, 1983), 386.
74. Waite, *Teaching Queer*, 133.
75. Brandt and Clinton, "Limits of the Local," 347.

2. Queer Appalachia and Queer Stories

1. Caleb Pendygraft, "Seeing Oddkin in the Prettiest Star's Appalachia," in *Appalachian Ecocriticism and the Paradox of Place*, ed. Jessica Cory and Laura Wright (Athens: The University of Georgia Press, 2023), 171–88.
2. Richard A. Straw and H. Tyler Blethen, eds., *High Mountains Rising: Appalachia and Time and Place* (Urbana: University of Illinois Press, 2004), 3.
3. Amy D. Clark and Nancy M. Hayward, eds., *Talking Appalachian: Voice, Identity, and Community* (Lexington: University Press of Kentucky, 2013), 1–2.
4. Jeff Biggers, *The United States of Appalachia: How Southern Mountaineers Brought Independence, Culture, and Enlightenment to America* (Berkeley: Catapult, 2007), xii–xiii.

5. Straw and Blethen, eds., *High Mountains Rising*, 18.
6. Ibid., 17.
7. Ibid., 34.
8. Catte, *What You Are Getting Wrong*, 71.
9. David E. Whisnant, *Modernizing the Mountaineer: People, Power, and Planning in Appalachia* (Knoxville: University of Tennessee Press, 1994), 126–55.
10. Catte, *What You Are Getting Wrong*, 11.
11. Ibid., 14–15.
12. Ronald D. Eller, *Uneven Ground: Appalachia since 1945* (Lexington: University Press of Kentucky, 2013), 3.
13. See Lauren Berlant and Michael Warner, "Sex in Public," in *Publics and Counterpublics*, ed. Michael Warner (Brooklyn, NY: Zone), 187–208; Judith Butler, *Gender Trouble: Feminism and the Subversion of Identity* (New York: Routledge, 1990); Robert McRuer, *Crip Theory: Cultural Signs of Queerness and Disability* (New York: New York University Press, 2006).
14. Berlant and Warner, "Sex in Public"; Butler, *Gender Trouble*; McRuer and Bérubé, *Crip Theory*.
15. Catte, *What You Are Getting Wrong*, 127.
16. I am not attempting to claim that to be Appalachian *is to leave Appalachia*. Instead, this was my perception of the area where I grew up and was intermittently homeless. I think the reason I had this perception was mainly due to the stereotypes that lingered from the Appalachian migration. As early as the 1930, then into the late '50s and beyond, Appalachians left their mountain jobs in order to find economic success in more urban, Midwestern cities like Cincinnati. My mom has even told me stories of how she experienced this herself as a young girl, around the age of five (circa 1970). She used to run the streets of Reading, a northern suburb of Cincinnati. For more on the Appalachian migration, see John Alexander Williams, *Appalachia: A History* (Chapel Hill: The University of North Carolina Press, 2003).
17. Anna Lowenhaupt Tsing, *The Mushroom at the End of the World: On the Possibility of Life in Capitalist Ruins* (Princeton, NJ: Princeton University Press, 2015), 157.
18. Barad, *Meeting the Universe Halfway*, 128.
19. Quantum physics has shown photons and electrons can affect one another when they're not in close proximity, being described as "spooky action at a distance" by Albert Einstein, Boris Podolsky, and Nathan Rosen, "Can Quantum-Mechanical Description of Physical Reality Be Considered Complete?," *Physical Review* 47, no. 10 (May 15, 1935): 777–80; "something like telepathy or backward-in-time causation,"

Timothy Morton, *Hyperobjects: Philosophy and ecology after the end of the world* (Minneapolis: University of Minnesota Press, 2013), 44–45. I'm not attempting to pretend I know exactly how quantum theory can explain this. I've attempted to read Einstein's arguments, and it reads like an experiment in module logic, which exposes contradictions in physics. My point here isn't to explicate Einstein's argument but to highlight that literacies deployed in factions, like quantum physics or, say, some banal example like Dungeons & Dragons, used to keep others *other* aren't getting us anywhere except more divided.

20. Bennett, *Vibrant*, 6, 116–17.

21. Haraway, *Staying*, 59.

22. Jeannette Armstrong, "Keepers of the Earth," in *Ecopsychology: Restoring the Earth, Healing the Mind*, ed. Theodore Roszak, Mary E. Gomes, and Allen D. Kanner (San Francisco: Sierra Club Books, 1995), 323.

23. Sandra G. Harding, *Feminism and Methodology: Social Science Issues* (Bloomington: Indiana University Press, 1987), 2–3.

24. Judith Butler, "Critically Queer," in *The Routledge Queer Studies Reader*, ed. Donald Eugene Hall, Annamarie Jagose with Andrea Bebell and Susan Potter (New York: Routledge, 2013), 21.

25. Judith Halberstam, *Female Masculinity* (Durham, NC: Duke University Press, 1998), 13.

26. See Manalansan, "The 'Stuff' of Archives," 97.

27. Patricia Sullivan and James E. Porter, *Opening Spaces: Writing Technologies and Critical Research Practices* (Greenwich, CT: Ablex, 1997), 27.

28. Jacqueline Jones Royster and Gesa Kirsch, *Feminist Rhetorical Practices: New Horizons for Rhetoric, Composition, and Literacy Studies* (Carbondale: Southern Illinois University Press, 2012).

29. Ellen Cushman, "The Rhetorician as an Agent of Social Change," *College Composition and Communication* 47, no. 1 (1996): 7–28, https://doi.org/10.2307/358271.

30. Katrina M. Powell and Pamela Takayoshi, "Accepting Roles Created for Us: The Ethics of Reciprocity," *College Composition and Communication* 54, no. 3 (2003): 394–422, https://doi.org/10.2307/3594171.

31. Ellen Lewin, "Who's Queer? What's Queer? Queer Anthropology through the Lens of Ethnography," *Cultural Anthropology* 31, no. 4 (2016): 598–606, https://doi.org/10.14506/ca31.4.08.

32. Jonathan Alexander, "Editorial Comment: Desiring Literacy," *College Composition and Communication* 69, no. 3 (2018): 529–33, http://www.jstor.org/stable/44784942.

33. Jacqueline Rhodes and Jonathan Alexander, *Techne: Queer Meditations on Writing the Self* (Logan: Computers and Composition Digital Press/Utah State University Press, 2015).

34. Alexander, "Editorial Comment," 532.

35. Lee Maracle, *Oratory: Coming to Theory* (North Vancouver, BC: Gallerie Publications, 1990), 7.

36. Malea Powell et al., "Our Story Begins Here: Constellating Cultural Rhetorics," *Enculturation: A Journal of Rhetoric, Writing, and Culture* 25 (2014): 1–28.

37. Gries, *Still Life*, 2015.

38. George Lakoff and Mark Johnson, *Metaphors We Live By* (Chicago: University of Chicago Press, 2003), 5.

39. Sylvia Scribner, "Literacy in Three Metaphors," *American Journal of Education* 93, no. 1 (1984): 6–21, https://doi.org/10.1086/443783.

40. Ibid., 9.

41. Ibid., 11.

42. Ibid., 12.

43. Ibid., 13.

44. Ibid., 14.

45. Lakoff and Johnson, *Metaphors*, 3.

46. Ahmed, *Cultural Politics*.

47. Lakoff and Johnson, *Metaphors*, 14.

48. Ibid., 200.

49. Ibid., 25.

3. Matters of the Closet

1. I discuss my rewrite of *folks* as *folx* and *folkways* as *folxways* more in depth in chapter 5. However, as I've noted in other publications, this is a rhetorical strategy to dislodge thinking around who can be considered "folks" and to what extent folkways exclude underrepresented peoples in communities such as those in rural America and Appalachia.

2. Steve Hogan and Lee Hudson, *Completely Queer: The Gay and Lesbian Encyclopedia* (New York: Henry Hold, 1998), 140.

3. Eve Kosofsky Sedgwick, *Epistemology of the Closet* (Berkeley: University of California Press, 1990), 71.

4. Michael Warner, *Publics and Counterpublics* (Cambridge, MA: MIT Press, 2002), 52.

5. Malinowitz, *Textual Orientations*.

6. Ibid., 266

7. Martha Marinara et al., "Cruising Composition Texts: Negotiating Sexual Difference in First-Year Readers," *College Composition and*

Communication 61, no. 2 (2009): 269–96; Jonathan Alexander, *Literacy, Sexuality, Pedagogy Theory and Practice for Composition Studies* (Logan: Utah State University Press, 2008); Connie Monson and Jacqueline Rhodes, "Risking Queer: Pedagogy, Performativity, and Desire in Writing Classrooms," *JAC* 24, no. 1 (2004): 79–91.

8. William P. Banks and Jonathan Alexander, "Queer Eye for the Comp Program: Toward a Queer Critique of WPA Work," in *The Writing Program Interrupted: Making Space for Critical Discourse*, ed. Donna Strickland and Jeanne Gunner (Portsmouth, NH: Boynton/Cook, 2009); Jonathan Alexander and Michelle Gibson, "Queer Composition(s): Queer Theory in the Writing Classroom," *JAC* 24, no. 1 (2004): 1–21.

9. Eric Darnell Pritchard, *Fashioning Lives: Black Queers and the Politics of Literacy* (Carbondale: Southern Illinois University Press, 2017), 45.

10. Barad, *Meeting the Universe Halfway*, 133.

11. I'm thinking of Sara Ahmed's, *Queer Phenomenology* (Durham, NC: Duke University Press Books, 2006), desk here. Chen's, *Animacies* (2012), rumination on a couch serves as another example.

12. Alexander, *Sexuality Literacies*; William P. Banks, "Written through the Body: Disruptions and 'Personal' Writing," *College English* 66, no. 1 (2003): 21–40; Martha Clark Cummings, "Someday This Pain Will Be Useful to You: Self-Disclosure and Lesbian and Gay Identity in the ESL Writing Classroom," *Journal of Basic Writing* 28, no. 1 (2009): 71–89, https://doi.org/10.37514/jbw-j.2009.28.1.05; Deborah Jean Kinder, "To Follow Your Heart: Coming Out through Literacy," *English Journal* 88, no. 2 (1998): 63, https://doi.org/10.2307/821692; Garret W. Nichols, "The Quiet Country Closet: Reconstructing a Discourse for Closeted Rural Experiences," *Present Tense: A Journal of Rhetoric in Society* 1, no. 3 (2013): n.p.; Lauren Smith, "Staging the Self: Queer Theory in the Composition Classroom," in *Straight with a Twist: Queer Theory and the Subject of Heterosexuality*, ed. Calvin Thomas (Urbana: University of Illinois Press, 2000), 68–85.

13. Cummings, "Someday This Pain."

14. Alexander, *Literacy, Sexuality, Pedagogy*, 106; Banks, "Written through the Body," 36.

15. Bennett, *Vibrant*, xvi.

16. Chen, *Animacies*.

17. Deborah Brant, *Literacy in American Lives* (New York: Cambridge University Press, 2001); Katherine Kelleher Sohn, *Whistlin' and Crowin' Women of Appalachia: Literacy Practices since College* (Carbondale: Southern Illinois University Press, 2006).

18. Alexander, *Literacy, Sexuality, Pedagogy*, 5.

19. Chen, *Animacies*, 11.

20. Hayes, *The Politics of Appalachian Rhetoric*, 115.

21. Ibid.

22. Sara Webb-Sunderhaus, "A Family Affair: Competing Sponsors of Literacy in Appalachian Students' Lives," *Community Literacy Journal* 2, no. 1 (2007): 5–24.

23. Barad, *Meeting the Universe Halfway*, 172.

24. Bennet, *Vibrant*, 112–13.

25. Hot Water Heaters—Temperature Regulation, 19 R.C.W. § 19.27A.060 (1983). My research here into water heaters may appear to be a detour, but in fact, I am allowing myself to listen to Justin's story and *its nonhuman* actors and respond accordingly. You could say that Justin's water heater is sponsoring my literacies learned in this chapter.

26. Thomas C. Erdmann et al., "Tap Water Burn Prevention: The Effect of Legislation," *Pediatrics* 88, no. 3 (1991): 572–77.

27. Guidelines for Construction and Equipment of Hospital and Medical Facilities, H. R. P. § 0905974 (1984); Uniform Federal Accessibility Standards (UFAS), 24 CFR § 8.32, (1988); American Correctional Association, *Adult Correctional Institutions*, 3rd ed. (Alexandria, VA: ACA, 1990).

28. International Plumbing Code, § 97/00 (1993).

29. Barad, *Meeting the Universe Halfway*, 178.

30. Ibid., 219.

31. Ibid., 235.

32. Robert McRuer, *Crip Theory: Cultural Signs of Queerness and Disability* (New York: New York University Press, 2006).

33. Alison Kafer, *Feminist, Queer, Crip* (Bloomington: Indiana University Press, 2013), 6.

34. Ibid., 17.

35. Catte, *What You Are Getting Wrong*; Barbara E. Smith, "Representing Appalachia: The Impossible Necessity of Appalachian Studies," in *Studying Appalachian Studies: Making the Path by Walking*, ed. Chad Berry, Phillip J. Obermiller, and Shaunna L. Scott (Urbana: University of Illinois Press, 2015), 42–61; John Alexander Williams, *Appalachia: A History* (Chapel Hill: The University of North Carolina Press, 2003).

36. Kafer, *Feminist, Queer, Crip*, 128.

4. Queer Affinities

1. Harper Douglas, "Etymology of Change," Online Etymology Dictionary, accessed August 11, 2023, https://www.etymonline.com/word/change; I recognize that Ireland is one among many genealogical histories of Appalachia.

2. Ahmed, *Queer Phenomenology*, 161.
3. Bennett, *Vibrant*, xiii.
4. Jonathan Alexander, *Literacy, Sexuality, Pedagogy Theory and Practice for Composition Studies* (Logan: Utah State University Press, 2008).
5. Brian Massumi, *Parables for the Virtual: Movement, Affect, Sensation* (Durham: Duke University Press, 2021).
6. Ibid., 35.
7. Ibid., 61.
8. Melissa Gregg and Gregory J. Seigworth, eds., *The Affect Theory Reader* (Durham, NC: Duke University Press, 2011), 2.
9. Ibid., 2.
10. Daniel Goleman, *Emotional Intelligence* (New York: Bantam, 1995), 83.
11. Ibid., 83.
12. Rob Bocchino, *Emotional Literacy: To Be a Different Kind of Smart* (Thousand Oaks, CA: Sage, 1999), 5.
13. Ibid., 11.
14. Melek Alemdar, "Examining the Emotional Literacy Skill Levels of High School Students," *Educational Policy Analysis and Strategic Research* 13, no. 2 (2018): 69–86, https://doi.org/10.29329/epasr.2018.143.4; Kerem Coskun and Yücel Oksuz, "Impact of Emotional Literacy Training on Students' Emotional Intelligence Performance in Primary Schools," *International Journal of Assessment Tools in Education* 6, no. 1 (2019): 36–47, https://doi.org/10.21449/ijate.503393.
15. Mark Amsler, *Affective Literacies: Writing and Multilingualism in the Late Middle Ages* (Turnhout, Belgium: Brepols, 2012), 103.
16. Albert Mehrabian, *Silent Messages* (Belmont, CA: Wadsworth, 1971); nonverbal communication has a large start in Mehrabian's work and can often be credited at the beginning of thinking about the body as equally important in understanding human interaction.
17. Kuby, Spector, and Thiel, *Posthuman and Literacy Education*, 186.
18. Ibid., 187.
19. I am not referencing any particular prior use of the term *pseudo-entities* here. In the last chapter, when I was looking at literacy matters, I examined actual *things* made up of matter. Literacy matters are, in fact, entities, or as object-oriented ontology would have put it, objects exist; this we know (see Timothy Morton, *Realist Magic: Objects, Ontology, Causality* [London: Open Humanities Press, 2013]). So when I say *pseudo-entities*, I mean that emotions and affects exist, but they aren't independent of the actors that experience them. They are *like* objects

but not fully their own—not in the way closets or water heaters exist on their own.

20. Micciche, *Doing Emotion*, 52.

21. Ibid., 74.

22. Micciche, "Staying with Emotion."

23. Laura R. Micciche, "Writing Material," *College English* 76, no. 6 (2014): 488–505, http://www.jstor.org/stable/24238199.

24. Chen, *Animacies*, 190.

25. Ahmed, *Cultural Politics*, 119.

26. Ibid., 8.

27. Ibid., 14.

28. Ibid., 155.

29. Haraway, *Staying*, 1.

30. JoAnn Snoderly, "West Virginia Again Leads Nation in Drug Overdose Deaths," November 29, 2018, https://www.wvnews.com/theet/news/west-virginia-again-leads-nation-in-drug-overdose-deaths/article_42d95e63-cd30-5e38-8ecd-cba357d923d9.html.

31. Sue L. T. McGregor, *Understanding and Evaluating Research: A Critical Guide* (Thousand Oaks, CA: Sage, 2018), 6.

32. Mary Sue MacNealy, *Strategies for Empirical Research in Writing* (Boston: Allyn and Bacon, 1999), 35, 45.

33. Eric Darnell Pritchard, *Fashioning Lives: Black Queers and the Politics of Literacy* (Carbondale: Southern Illinois University Press, 2017).

34. Ibid., 129.

35. Ann E. Berthoff, *The Making of Meaning: Metaphors, Models, and Maxims for Writing Teachers* (Upper Montclair, NJ: Boynton/Cook, 1981), 31.

36. Ibid.

37. MacNealy, *Strategies for Empirical Research*, 35, 45; 10th General Synod, "A Pronouncement: Civil Liberates without Discrimination Related to Affectional or Sexual Preferences" (Minneapolis: United Church of Christ, July 27, 1975), https://openandaffirming.org/wp-content/uploads/2013/09/1975-A-PRONOUNCEMENT-CIVIL-LIBERTIES-WITHOUT-DISCRIMINATION.pdf. The General Synod is a legislative order within the church. Their role is to pass church bylaws and issue doctrine.

38. 25th General Synod, "In Support of Equal Marriage Rights for All" (Atlanta: United Church of Christ, July 4, 2005), 1, https://www.ucc.org/wp-content/uploads/2021/01/marriage-equality-1.pdf.

39. Ibid., 3.

40. Ibid., 5.

41. Steven Angelides, *A History of Bisexuality* (Chicago: University of Chicago Press, 2001).

42. Juana María Rodríguez, "Queer Politics, Bisexual Erasure," *Lambda Nordica* 21, no. 1–2 (2016): 169–82; Nancy Marcus, "Bridging Bisexual Erasure in LGBT-Rights Discourse and Litigation," *Michigan Journal of Gender and Law* 22, no. 2 (2015): 291–344, https://doi.org/10.36641/mjgl.22.2.bridging.

43. Sara Ahmed, *Living a Feminist Life* (Durham, NC: Duke University Press, 2017), 123.

44. Barad, *Meeting the Universe Halfway*, 142.

45. Alexander, *Literacy, Sexuality, Pedagogy*, 5.

5. Carrying Mountains to the Sea

1. The *TS Kennedy* is no longer at MMA at the time of publication.

2. Rebecca R. Scott, *Removing Mountains: Extracting Nature and Identity in the Appalachian Coalfields* (Minneapolis: University Minnesota Press, 2010).

3. Caleb Pendygraft, "Comin' Out the Broom Closet: Appalachian Pagans and Their Queer Future Worlding," *Journal of Appalachian Studies* 28, no. 1 (April 1, 2022): 49–69, https://doi.org/10.5406/23288612.28.1.04.

4. Harper Douglas, "Etymology of Folk," Online Etymology Dictionary, accessed August 11, 2023, https://www.etymonline.com/word/folk.

5. William H. Turner, *The Harlan Renaissance: Stories of Black Life in Appalachian Coal Towns* (Morgantown: West Virginia University Press), 2021.

6. Susan Pepper, Press, accessed August 11, 2023, https://susanpepper.com/press.

7. Eliot Wigginton, *Foxfire* (New York: Doubleday, 1975).

8. Luke Manget, *Ginseng Diggers: A History of Root and Herb Gathering in Appalachia* (Lexington: University Press of Kentucky, 2022).

9. David A. Taylor, "The Fight against Ginseng Poaching in the Great Smoky Mountains," *Smithsonian Magazine*, April 21, 2016.

10. Ava DuVernay, *13th*, Kandoo Films (2016), Netflix.com.

11. Patrick Huber, "Red Necks and Red Bandanas: Appalachian Coal Miners and the Coloring of Union Identity, 1912–1936," *Western Folklore* 65, no. 1/2 (2006): 195–210.

About the Author

Caleb Pendygraft is an associate professor of humanities and writes on and questions the intersections of literacies in Appalachia, new materialisms, queerness, and nonhumans. He has published multiple articles and chapters that examine queerness in Appalachia more generally and is currently thinking through Appalachian paganism as a means to reimagine our relationship with the region.

Appalachian Futures
Black, Native, and Queer Voices

Series editors
Annette Saunooke Clapsaddle, Davis Shoulders, and Crystal Wilkinson

This book series gives voice to Black, Native, Latinx, Asian, Queer, and other nonwhite or ignored identities within the Appalachian region.

Black Freedom Struggle in Urban Appalachia
Edited by J. Z. Bennett, Christy L. McGuire, Lori Delale-O'Connor, T. Elon Dancy II, and Sabina Vaught

Affrilachia: Testimonies
Chris Aluka Berry with Kelly Elaine Navies and Maia A. Surdam

No Son of Mine: A Memoir
Jonathan Corcoran

To Belong Here: A New Generation of Queer, Trans, and Two-Spirit Appalachian Writers
Edited by Rae Garringer

Tar Hollow Trans: Essays
Stacy Jane Grover

Deviant Hollers: Queering Appalachian Ecologies for a Sustainable Future
Edited by Zane McNeill and Rebecca Scott

Reading, Writing, and Queer Survival: Affects, Matterings, and Literacies across Appalachia
Caleb Pendygraft

Appalachian Ghost: A Photographic Reimagining of the Hawk's Nest Tunnel Disaster
Raymond Thompson Jr.